THE ULTIMATE *Young and the Restless* TRIVIA BOOK

THE ULTIMATE
Young and the
Restless
TRIVIA BOOK

GERARD J. WAGGETT

RENAISSANCE BOOKS

Los Angeles

Library of Congress Catalog Card Number: 00-102824
ISBN: 1-58063-145-2

10 9 8 7 6 5 4 3 2 1

Cover photos of Laura Lee Bell, Eric Braeden, Eileen Davidson, Melody Scott Thomas, Shemar Moore, and Joshua Morrow courtesy of Albert Ortega/Moonglow. Cover photos of Peter Bergman and Jeanne Cooper courtesy of Sue Schneider/Moonglow.

Design by Susan Shankin
Typeset by Amanda Tan

Published by Renaissance Books
Distributed by St. Martin's Press
Manufactured in the United States of America
First Edition

For Gretchen Young,
who has set so much in motion

Contents

QUIZZES

Acknowledgments

AS ALWAYS, my first thank you goes to my editor, Brenda Scott Royce, who continues to allow me to make a living doing two things I enjoy—watching soap operas and writing. I am also grateful for the extension and the e-mail during those last few weeks, which kept me focused and sane as the book spun a little out of control.

Secondly, I need to express my gratitude to my agents, Frank Coffey and Frank Weimann, who pull these book deals together with such ease and worry about the little details that would drive me crazy.

Thirdly, Sue Schneider of Moonglow, Incorporated, provided the photos used in the book. To her and her stable of photographers, thanks for the added touch these pictures give the book.

As my dedication notes, I would also like to thank Gretchen Young, a former editor of mine, who did indeed set all this into motion when she bought my first book, *The Soap Opera Book of Lists*. She subsequently signed me up for four more soap opera books, helping me turn a lifelong dream of publishing a book into a real career. She has been an amazing woman with whom to work and a continued source of support.

When it comes to the issue of continued support, my family immediately comes to mind—namely my mother and father, Barbara and Frederick Waggett. I would also like to single out my Aunt Margaret Connolly; my uncles Eddie and Jackie Connolly; my cousin Mabel Waggett; my brothers Frederick, Michael, and Kevin; and their wives Keri, Christine, and Julie. And for a book about *The Young and the*

Restless, for that extra something they bring to my life, I'd like to mention my brothers' young: Taylor, Norma, Ava, and Matthew.

My friends also help me, sometimes in ways that they don't even realize. As such, I need to thank: Paul Bonaceto, Don Casali, Robin DiCarlo, Chris Leland, the Montgomerys (Derek, Roseanne, Dylan, and Aidan), Jeffery McGraw, Beth Pratt, the Richards family (Amanda, Jack, Kevin, Jay, Katie, Corinne, and Tina), Louise Shaffer, the Skippers (Pete, Mary, Kassie, Lani, and Petey), Jerry Stonehouse, and last but by no means least, the Walshes (Mike, Connie, Jamie, Renée, Brendan, Brigitte, and Marita).

Introduction

IN 1998, *The Young and the Restless* celebrated three important anniversaries: its twenty-fifth year on television, Jeanne Cooper's twenty-fifth year playing Katherine Chancellor, and the show's tenth year as daytime's top-rated soap opera. All three milestones were honored with a storyline that dug deep into the show's history. When Jill Abbott (Jess Walton) needed a place to live, Katherine invited her to stay at the Chancellor mansion, a gesture that harkened back to the pair's long ago friendship. That friendship had deteriorated into a bitter rivalry after Jill slept with Katherine's husband. This time around, Jill's gratitude gave way to anger when she discovered evidence that the Chancellor mansion might actually belong to her. The ensuing legal battle, the latest round in a decades-old feud, epitomized the key not only to *Y&R*'s longevity but also to its continued popularity.

Crucial to the series's success is its consistency. Although critics can fault the show for inconsistency with certain plot details—Jill's son Billy was born several years after her grandson Phillip, but now Billy has been rapidly aged to be several years older than Phillip, who grows in real time—as a whole, the show remains impressively consistent. The Katherine/Jill feud can still take center stage twenty-odd years after it began because *The Young and the Restless* is basically the same show it was in 1974. Most of daytime's other soaps have, to some degree or another, reinvented themselves over the years, some more successfully than others. *General Hospital* soared to its phenomenal streak of popularity in the late 1970s to early '80s by shifting the focus from doctors and nurses to gangsters and secret agents. *Days of Our Lives,* which thrived as a sexually provocative psychodrama under *Y&R*

creator Bill Bell's pen, has morphed into the fantasy realm of Satanic possession and mind control. During the mid-'80s, when Y&R was struggling to rebuild its audience, it did veer off track by introducing the sort of mob storyline that had taken over daytime, but it was a short diversion.

For the most part, The Young and the Restless has never needed to reinvent itself. Yes, it experienced a ratings dip in the early '80s, but that was caused by a time slot change and exodus of favorite faces rather than by anything the show was doing "wrong." From the very beginning, Bill Bell had the vision of what it would take to create a hit show. The show's initial ratings may have been disappointing (it ranked seventeenth out of seventeen), but the show picked up steam in a relatively short span of time. Within three years of its debut, The Young and the Restless was the third most popular soap on daytime.

The show climbed its way up in the ratings by weaving together provocative storylines with social issues, a combination that Bell knew from experience was not guaranteed to work. Another World, which he had co-created with Irna Phillips in the 1960s, failed to entice viewers with its controversial blend of illegal abortion and murder, taking years to finally carve out an audience. Y&R, on the other hand, benefited by debuting a decade later. By the early '70s, TV was finally owning up to its sexuality. Y&R, which distinguished itself from other soaps with its dark, atmospheric lighting, also set itself apart from its competitors by exploring the darker side of sexual behavior. Jill Foster (Brenda Dickson) was nearly lured into prostitution; Katherine Chancellor was regularly "serviced" by her stable boys; and Lorie Brooks (Jaime Lyn Bauer) fell in love with her own half-brother. But Y&R was out to do more than titillate the viewers. The show gave its characters greater depth by using them as vehicles for exploring social issues. Jill's terminally ill father was put out of his misery by her mother; Katherine, an alcoholic, admitted her addiction at an AA meeting; and Lorie's mother discovered a lump in her breast requiring a mastectomy.

Despite the occasional detour into crime drama, The Young and the Restless has held steady to its identity, mixing provocative romance with a social conscience. Nikki Reed (Melody Thomas Scott) killed her father when he tried to rape her; two years later, she met Victor Newman (Eric Braeden) while stripping at a nightclub. Jill Foster married millionaire John Abbott (Jerry Douglas), then slept with his son Jack (Terry Lester); John subsequently married a woman with AIDS. Phyllis Romalotti (Sandra Nelson) broke out the handcuffs for a sadomasochistic romp with Michael Baldwin (Christian LeBlanc), the attorney who had sexually harassed his associate, Christine Blair (Lauralee Bell).

In addition to remaining true to its original vision, Y&R stays on top because of its long-term storytelling. The feud between Katherine and Jill is often cited as the longest-running storyline in daytime history, twenty-five years with more to come. At this writing, it looks as though Jill is developing an alcohol problem, a story twist that will no doubt incorporate Katherine's own alcoholism and lead the pair down yet another corridor of their complex relationship.

Viewers, however, will more than likely have to wait a little while for that plot to reach its peak. Bill Bell and Kay Alden (who wrote Y&R with Bell for twenty-four years and has been flying solo since 1998) have long displayed their own patience in hitting the high moments. The pair have left fans waiting more than fifteen years for John Abbott to finally learn that Ashley (Eileen Davidson) is not his biological daughter. If the feud between Katherine and Jill is daytime's longest running storyline, Ashley's paternity must be daytime's longest kept secret. If you pressed Bell on why it has taken this long for the truth to surface, he would probably answer that every story unfolds in its own time and that the moment for John to learn the truth simply has not yet come.

Although such pacing frustrates some viewers, Bell and Alden don't just spin stories long, they spin them wide as well. Y&R doesn't jump from plot twist to plot twist. Characters live with each revelation and catastrophe thrown their way in something that approximates real time. This style of storytelling gives each twist that much more weight, that much greater a sense of payoff. The Abbotts regaining control of Jabot Cosmetics in 1999 felt like that much greater of a victory because it had been lost to them for ten whole years.

In addition to increasing that sense of payoff, slowing down the pacing prevents the characters from burning out. Writers don't rush through a dozen plotlines during an actor's first three-year contract. Katherine and Jill have been on the Genoa City canvas for more than twenty-six years, but the writers can still find new story material for the pair—individually and together—because the two have not already exhausted every plot permutation. Likewise, Paul Williams (Doug Davidson), Nikki Reed Newman, Victor Newman, and Jack Abbott have each been around for at least twenty years and rarely want for airtime.

Because soap fans tune in not just for the plotlines but for the characters, keeping long-term favorites such as Katherine and Jill front and center has given *The Young and the Restless* a greater level of stability—exactly what a soap opera needs when it is sitting on top of the ratings.

Genoa City Chronicle

IN **1966,** As the World Turns head writer Bill Bell signed on to write the new NBC serial Days of Our Lives, which was already in danger of cancellation. Bell's combination of topical storylines and controversial subject matter helped push the show all the way to number one in the ratings. CBS, whose As the World Turns had been temporarily dislodged from its summit, wanted Bell back on their team. The network offered him the chance to create his own soap opera, a show that would bring in the younger viewers, who were finally being recognized as a target audience.

1973: Corday Productions, which produced Days of Our Lives, was none too happy with the idea of losing the head writer who had brought Days to its height of popularity. A lawsuit was filed to prevent Bell from leaving. The matter was settled out of court with Bell agreeing to remain at Days for three more years, during which time he would also be working on Y&R.

In the beginning, creator Bill Bell and his wife, Lee, had toyed with calling the show The Innocent Years, as it would focus on young romance. When the Bells took a good look at America's youth, however, they could not ignore rising rates in drug addiction, criminal activity, and out-of-wedlock pregnancy. The Innocent Years suddenly sounded rather naive. The Young and the Restless would prove a far more provocative and enticing lure for young viewers.

On March 26, TV audiences saw the very first episode of The Young and the Restless. The first installment featured a scene with Dr. Brad Eliot (Tom Hallick), mugged and beaten, arriving in Genoa City on a truck.

The Young and the Restless **creators Bill Bell and Lee Phillip Bell.**

© *Sue Schneider, Moonglow Photos*

Lee Crawford, as waitress Sally McGuire, spoke the first line: "Kind of a drag, isn't it? Stuck in a place like Genoa City. God, I feel so restless."

Y&R quickly distinguished itself from other soap operas with its look, opting for moodier lighting, something closer to what people would see in feature films. Executive producer John Conboy himself took a personal interest in the lighting. Also like something out of a film, characters would occasionally burst into song. *Y&R* further distinguished itself through its dialogue, which would contain frank but tasteful discussions about pre-marital sex and related issues.

Despite its distinctive sights and sounds, when it came down to basic storytelling, *Y&R* followed the classic soap opera construction that had worked for ratings winners such as *Days* and *World Turns:* two families—one wealthy, the other struggling—intertwined by romance. The couple linking the wealthy Brooks family and the middle class Fosters was Chris Brooks (Trish Stewart) and medical student Bill "Snapper" Foster (William Grey Espy). During the show's early days, their romance was a focal point of the action. Lee Phillip Bell, who once hosted a talk show in the Chicago area, encouraged Bell to include socially relevant storylines in the show. In response, Bell crafted a story in which Chris Brooks was raped by George Curtis (played by future daytime superstar Tony Geary). It was the first non-marital rape shown on daytime. More than simply examining the emotional ramifications of the act, *Y&R* explored the legal side as well, including the shocking but painfully realistic plot twist wherein the rapist was found not guilty.

1974: By the end of the show's first year on the air, Bill Bell was so disgusted by the ratings that he wanted CBS to pull the plug. Although it started out at the very bottom of the charts, it began building steadily, picking up a million viewers.

The character of Katherine Chancellor (Jeanne Cooper), who had been introduced in late 1973, crossed paths with Jill Foster (then played by Brenda Dickson). Katherine hired Jill as her personal hairdresser and companion. A triangle developed between Jill, Katherine, and Katherine's husband, Phillip (John Considine, later Donnelly Rhodes). Phillip's affair with Jill, which hit Katherine as a double betrayal, began a feud between the two women that has become not only the show's but also daytime's longest-running storyline. Ultimately, the feud inadvertently cost Phillip Chancellor his life and ruined several of Kay and Jill's subsequent marriages. Twenty-six years later, the battle is still raging, with Jill and Katherine once again sharing the very mansion where their feud began.

1975: The show's ratings finally began to soar. Just two years after its debut, *The Young and the Restless* had climbed to number three in popularity among the daytime soaps. Ironically, the soaps that kept *Y&R* out of the top spot were the long-running ratings champion *As the World Turns,* which Bill Bell had written during its peak of popularity in the 1960s, and

Another World, which Bell had co-created with Irna Phillips. Right behind *Y&R* was *Days of Our Lives*, which Bell was still headwriting at the time.

1976: One of the highlights of the Summer Olympics in Montreal was the gold medal–winning long program by Romanian gymnast Nadia Comaneci. Comaneci performed her routine to the theme song from *The Young and the Restless*. Record producers capitalized on Comaneci's popularity by releasing the instrumental piece (performed by Barry DeVorzon and Perry Botkin Jr.) as a single under the title "Nadia's Theme." It climbed all the way to number seven on Billboard's Hot 100 chart and remains the only daytime soap opera theme to hit the top ten on the pop charts.

A clip from the show, featuring Brenda Dickson (JILL FOSTER) and Beau Kazer (BROCK REYNOLDS), was used in the Robert DeNiro film *Taxi Driver*. The romantic scene between Jill and Brock compelled DeNiro's deranged character to smash his foot right into the TV set.

1977: In 1976, while writing *Days of Our Lives*, Bill Bell broke one of the more controversial daytime taboos by introducing a bisexual woman with feelings for its lead heroine, Julie Williams (Susan Seaforth Hayes, who would play Lauren Fenmore's mother JoAnna in the mid-1980s). A year later, Bell pushed the envelope even further, having Katherine Chancellor, an established character on *Y&R*, develop feelings for another woman, in this case her new assistant, Joann Curtis (Kay Heberle). Katherine was still reeling from Phillip's infidelity and subsequent death. The overweight Joann had her own problems, her husband having left her for a younger, thinner woman. The audience did not take well to this storyline. Many straight fans complained that the show was tackling this issue at all; gays complained that the show wasn't tackling it hard enough. Protesters charged that the storyline was all talk and didn't dare show any physical contact between the women. Bill Bell often says that Katherine's lesbian dalliance cost him a million viewers. Within one year, the ratings slipped from 8.7 to 7.8. A quick resolution was called for. As the two women were preparing to leave on vacation, where they would presumably consummate their relationship, Katherine's religious son Brock (Beau Kazer) shamed them into calling things off. Joann went back to her husband, and Katherine soon entered into a sexually charged relationship with a younger man.

1978: Two of the show's longest running and most popular characters were introduced: Nikki Reed (originally played by Erica Hope) and Paul Williams (Doug Davidson). Although the two characters have matured over the years, they were originally used to illustrate one of the dangerous repercussions of the sort of promiscuity Y&R had been accused of promoting. Daytime legend has Paul infecting Nikki with gonorrhea, but Doug Davidson told *Soap Opera Digest* that it was actually the other way around: Nikki gave it to Paul.

1979: When Lynne Richter, who had taken over the role of Chris Brooks Foster, told the producers that she was expecting a child, they decided to write the pregnancy into Chris's storyline—the first time they had done so for an actress on the show. One of the scenes called for Chris's husband, Dr. Snapper Foster (David Hasselhoff) to bring home a device that would amplify the baby's heartbeat so that she could hear it. A few days before that scene was to be taped, Richter took the instrument home to practice using it. While doing so, she discovered that she was going to have twins. Because of the long work hours, tight schedules, and child labor laws, twins are often employed to play small children on television. As a result, producer John Conboy convinced Richter to allow her girls to play Chris's daughter.

1980: On February 1, 1980, CBS canceled one of its longest-running serials, the twenty-nine-year-old *Love of Life.* Rather than launch a brand new soap opera, CBS wanted to fill the vacated time slot with another half hour of *The Young and the Restless,* its top-rated soap at the time. Although reluctant to mess with a formula that was working, Bill Bell agreed to expand Y&R from thirty minutes to a full hour. Bell had, in fact, turned down repeated requests by the network to expand the show to an hour since the mid-1970s when the show first began proving itself a ratings powerhouse. On February 4, the first hourlong episode of Y&R debuted. Along with the expansion came a new time slot. The show, which had been running from 12:30 to 1:00 E.S.T., now began at 1:00, putting it head to head with ABC's *All My Children,* daytime's second most popular soap at the time. The time change cost the show more than a million viewers.

1981: General Hospital hit an incredible peak of popularity by injecting science fiction into its format: a mad scientist tried to freeze the world with a weather controlling machine. *Y&R* meanwhile was struggling to regain its ratings loss, but it was too strongly rooted in reality to go anywhere near such a plotline. So while the rest of daytime was dabbling in science fiction, *Y&R* leaned toward high-tech Gothic drama. Victor Newman (Eric Braeden), who was far more villainous in his early days, kidnapped his wife Julia's lover, Michael Scott (Nick Benedict), and imprisoned the man in a fallout shelter beneath the Newman ranch. The fallout shelter was equipped with two-way monitor screens, which not only allowed Victor to keep tabs on his prisoner, but also to torture the man with images of Victor making love to Julia (Meg Bennett).

1982: Y&R suffered a dual loss. John Conboy, who had been producing the show from day one, left to produce the fledgling soap *Capitol.* He was replaced by H. Wesley Kenney, an Emmy-winning director from *Days of Our Lives,* who immediately changed the show's look by abandoning the moody darkness for a level of lighting he felt would better show off the incredible sets and beautiful stars.

Jaime Lyn Bauer (LORIE BROOKS), who had played the show's lead heroine since 1973, decided that it was time to leave. Bill Bell had recast each of Lorie's three sisters at least once during the previous nine years, but he was tired of finding new actors to take over established roles. It made more sense to him to bring in someone new to play someone new. Within a few months, and much to CBS's dismay, Bell wrote off not only Lorie Brooks but her family, and the majority of his other leading family, the Fosters, as well. In their place, he beefed up families around Paul Williams and Jack Abbott (Terry Lester), who had been on the canvas since 1980. As Bell had once done with the middle class Fosters and wealthy Brookses, Bell connected the middle class Williams clan with the rich Abbott dynasty through romance, linking Paul's sister Patty (Lilibet Stern) with Jack Abbott.

1983: Brenda Dickson, who had left the show in 1980 to become a full-time wife, reclaimed the role of Jill Foster. Her return helped bring back a number of the fans who had been lost when the show changed time slots. The show picked up more than a million fans, bringing its ratings all the way back to where they had been before the show expanded to an hour.

1984: When Jeanne Cooper decided to undergo a facelift, she naturally talked to Bill Bell first. As her boss, he had a right to know about any decision that would radically change her onscreen image. Bell not only decided to incorporate Cooper's facelift into Katherine's storyline, he decided to take his cameras where no soap opera had ever gone before—into a real-life operating room. Cooper agreed to let *Y&R* tape her facelift and use scenes from the procedure on the air. Happening long before the widespread availability of cable channels like Discovery, Katherine's storyline gave many viewers at home their first glimpse inside a real-life operating room.

When Nikki Reed (Melody Thomas Scott) agreed to marry Victor Newman, the producers realized that this was going to be a major event in the show's history. They pulled out all the stops, spending twenty-five thousand dollars on Nikki's gown alone. Making the event all the more special for longtime viewers, a number of past cast members returned. Even though the wedding was destined to be a ratings high point, the producers did not save the union for a sweeps month but instead had them marry during the summer, on July 17.

1985: By the mid-1980s, the success of gangster storylines on the top-rated *General Hospital* led most of daytime to follow suit, including *Y&R*. *Y&R* took a unique approach to the "hero going undercover" convention: African-American lawyer Tyrone Jackson (Phil Morris) posed as a white man in order to infiltrate the mob. The storyline also included a controversial but unconsummated romance between Tyrone and mob princess Alana Anthony (Amy Gibson). Visitors to the *Y&R* set clamored to see Phil Morris in person, making him feel at times like a zoo exhibit.

1986: Bill Bell moved himself and his family from Chicago to Los Angeles, where *Y&R* is produced, allowing him a hands-on approach to the show. *The Young and the Restless* made its first move to overthrow *General Hospital* as the most popular soap opera on daytime television. For nine straight weeks during the summer, *Y&R* was ranked number one. A topical storyline exploring the connection between rock music and teen pregnancy was credited with drawing in younger viewers who were out of school for the summer.

1987: Seldom does a star as popular and as integral to the plotline as Brenda Dickson (JILL ABBOTT) simply get fired. But trouble had long been brewing between Dickson and the powers that be. Her desire for perfection earned her a reputation on the set for being difficult to work with. More than simply concerning herself with the delivery of her lines, Dickson worried about her hair, her wardrobe, the camera angles, and the lighting. When any of those factors failed to live up to her high standards, she had no compunctions about walking off the set. In June, the trouble between Dickson and the producers reached fever pitch. Not only was Dickson arguing about the way Jill was being presented, she herself was suffering from a painful urinary tract infection. When she asked for permission to go home, Bill Bell reportedly told her that if she left the set, she would be fired. Despite the warning, Dickson left. The next day, she learned that Bell had not been bluffing; she received notification that she had been fired. Dickson retaliated by filing a $10 million lawsuit against Bill Bell and Columbia Pictures, which produced the soap. Dickson's suit contended she had been wrongfully terminated and that the producers had actively demeaned her reputation so as to prevent her from finding employment elsewhere. Dickson eventually dropped the lawsuit.

1988: The opening credits were changed: Line drawings of the varied cast members were replaced with filmed images of the actors.

Y&R ultimately dethroned *General Hospital* as the number-one ranked daytime soap. On December 26, *Y&R* began its as-yet uninterrupted run. Ironically, executive producer H. Wesley Kenney had recently left *Y&R* to work his magic on *General Hospital.*

1989: During most of the '80s, Terry Lester dominated Y&R as the show's resident bad boy, Jack Abbott. As the decade was winding down, Lester told *Soap Opera Digest* that Jack had "dwindled from leading man to second banana." In an odd twist, he didn't see his position threatened by such fellow lead actors as Eric Braeden (VICTOR NEWMAN) or Don Diamont (BRAD CARLTON) but by Lauralee Bell, who played Christine "Cricket" Blair and who just happened to be boss Bill Bell's daughter. Lester believed that Jack's airtime was pared back to make more room for Cricket's romances and social issue storylines. In a surprise move, Lester quit—and none too quietly. Bill Bell dismissed Lester's claims as "ridiculous." Peter Bergman, recently let go from *All My Children,* took over the role of Jack Abbott, while Lester nabbed the highly coveted role of Mason Capwell on *Santa Barbara.* Lester and Bell eventually made peace with one another.

1990: Although Y&R had never taken the cameras further from the studio than San Francisco, the decision was made to head to the island of Bermuda for a pivotal moment in the George Rawlins murder mystery. Paul Williams, who had been arrested for Rawlins's murder, faked his own death, then gaslighted George's widow, Cassandra (Nina Arvesen) when she headed to Bermuda with the real killer, hit man Adrian Hunter (Mark Derwin). Bell decided that the Bermuda remote would not only accent the importance of this arc in the storyline but the island scenery would also be a nice treat for the viewers, airing as it would during the middle of winter.

The Bermuda remote went so well that the producers took the cameras on the road again, this time heading to Hawaii for the long-anticipated wedding of Danny Romalotti (Michael Damian) and Christine Blair (Lauralee Bell). Bill Bell finally decided to step in front of the cameras, appearing as an extra at the hotel in which all the characters were staying. Despite his clout as the executive producer, creator, and head writer, Bell's scene was cut from the show—a fact he did not discover until he sat down to watch the episode.

1991: After Sheila Carter (Kimberlin Brown) miscarried Dr. Scott Grainger's (Peter Barton) baby, she worried about losing him to his ex-wife, Lauren (Tracey E. Bregman), whom he had also impregnated. Sheila kidnapped

Brenda Dickson
was fired in 1987.

© Albert Ortega,
Moonglow Photos

Lauren's son as soon as he was born and replaced him with a black market baby who later died. Although a powerful moment in the storyline, the baby's death broke a vow Bill Bell had made more than twenty years before, when he was head writing *Days of Our Lives*. Bell was so moved by the audience's distress over the death of a child on that show, he swore he would never kill another child in one of his scripts.

Y&R staged its first full-scale masquerade ball, which served as the grand finale to golddigger/wife killer David Kimble's (Michael Corbett) reign of terror. Kay Alden, who was co-headwriting the show at the time, described the ball to *Soap Opera Weekly* as being "as lavish as Y&R has ever done." Although the ball looked incredible and boosted the ratings, because of the work involved, Alden noted, "It'll be a long time before we do another masquerade ball." The ball ended with one of the most unconventional endings to any major soap opera character: David was crushed to death in a trash compactor.

1992: Despite all her crimes, Sheila Carter had proved immensely popular with the fans. Despite that popularity, Bill Bell didn't see a believable way to keep the character on the show. So, in a rare move for daytime at the time, Sheila was transplanted from Genoa City into *Bold and the Beautiful*'s Los Angeles, where she proceeded to disrupt the lives of that show's core family, the Forresters. Up to this point, there had been little interaction between the two shows. Lauren Fenmore (Tracey E. Bregman), it was later revealed, was a longtime family friend to the Forresters; she headed out to Los Angeles for a business deal with them. The crossover confrontation between Lauren and Sheila (which turned out to be a dream the first time around) not only boosted *Y&R*'s ratings but helped *B&B* climb as high as number two for several weeks. So successful was the crossover that it continued until 1995, when Lauren was relocated to *B&B* permanently.

On October 29, CBS aired the five thousandth episode of *The Young and the Restless*. To mark the occasion, the network dedicated Studio 43 at CBS Television Studio, where the show is taped, to both *The Young and the Restless* and its creator Bill Bell—the first time the network has ever made such a dedication. The city of Los Angeles also marked the occasion by proclaiming October 29, 1992, William J. Bell Day.

Y&R made national news when a fight erupted backstage between Peter Bergman and Eric Braeden. The confrontation began during the taping of a scene in which Braeden felt that Victor should have the last line. Bergman's suggestion that Braeden stick to the script did not sit too well with Braeden. When Braeden showed up at Bergman's dressing room the next day to further discuss the matter, the discussion turned into an argument, which progressed into a physical fight. Both Bergman and Braeden pressed criminal charges, which they later dropped. They also issued public apologies to one another.

1993: After months of being presumed dead, Victor Newman sent invitations to his friends, adversaries, business partners, and family members bringing them together at the Colonnade Room for a mysterious meeting. That confrontation, in which they all learned that Victor was indeed alive, helped *The Young and the Restless* score a 9.1 in the ratings—the highest rating any soap has scored during daytime hours in recent years.

1994: At CBS's request, Y&R ventured into primetime for the first time, airing a special episode on Thursday evening, March 3. Some critics panned the episode for upping the sex factor—one of the scenes cited found a leotard-clad Lauralee Bell (Christine) working a chest press in her home gym. The episode ended with April Lynch (Cynthia [Eilbacher] Jordan) stabbing her abusive husband to death, a plot twist that launched a long-term story arc. The episode garnered an 10.2 in the ratings, an impressive step up from the 8.5 average for the daytime episodes that aired that week. Three additional primetime episodes were produced in the ensuing years.

1995: The producers and writers of the Dick Van Dyke mystery series *Diagnosis Murder* decided to set one of its episodes against the background of a daytime soap opera. The natural choice was *The Young and the Restless*—not only because both series aired on CBS, but also because Victoria Rowell, who played Drucilla Winters on Y&R, was also a regular on *Diagnosis Murder.* In the course of the episode, titled "Death in the Daytime," Rowell's *Diagnosis* character, Amanda Bentley, won a walk-on role on Y&R only to discover that someone was threatening the lives of varied cast members. Eric Braeden (VICTOR NEWMAN), Melody Thomas Scott (NIKKI REED), Lauralee Bell (CHRISTINE BLAIR), Jeanne Cooper (KATHERINE CHANCELLOR), J. Eddie Peck (COLE HOWARD), Heather Tom (VICTORIA NEWMAN), and Doug Davidson (PAUL WILLIAMS) guest-starred as themselves. In the episode, one of Rowell's *Diagnosis Murder* cast mates joked that Amanda looked like the actress who played Dru on Y&R.

Y&R, which had distinguished itself from other soaps in the '70s with its minimally attired actors and actresses, took an even more provocative step. During a bedroom scene between Paul and Christine, Doug Davidson became the first soap actor to bare his derriere on daytime.

1996: *The Young and the Restless* had been the overall top-rated soap opera since 1988 but never once in the all-important demographic of women aged eighteen to forty-nine, the audience advertisers care most about reaching. That honor usually belonged to ABC's *All My Children.* Fueled by a number of high-powered storylines (Nick and Sharon's

Evil nurse Sheila Carter was transplanted from *The Young and
the Restless* to *The Bold and the Beautiful.*

© *Albert Ortega, Moonglow Photos*

romance, Jack Abbott's marriage to Luan Volien, Olivia's AIDS scare, and the machinations of Phyllis Romalotti), the show finally won over the prized demographic during the February sweeps.

1997: On March 3, Bill Bell turned seventy. Via a billboard, CBS wished "Happy Birthday to the Father of Soap Operas."

The 1996 primetime special episode and its follow-up—featuring Victor's shooting and airlift to the hospital—helped *The Young and the Restless* snag its first Directors Guild Award. Although *Y&R* had dominated the directing category at the Daytime Emmy Awards, it had not fared nearly so well with the DGAs, which had begun to include soaps in 1991.

1998: The Young and the Restless marked its silver anniversary with a coffee table book detailing and illustrating the show's history, a primetime episode, a soundtrack CD, and a storyline that Bill Bell himself described to *Soap Opera Digest* as "the most powerful and compelling love story [the show has] ever done." He was talking about Nikki's shooting and her subsequent "deathbed" wedding to Victor, a reunion for which the fans had been clamoring since the couple broke up ten years previously. The storyline was so important to Bill Bell that he personally wrote the promos that would air on CBS.

On March 26, the twenty-fifth anniversary of the debut episode, producers buried a time capsule in the main driveway of CBS Television Studios in Hollywood. Packed inside the capsule were scripts from that first episode as well as the twenty-fifth anniversary episode; the latter was signed by all the actors and producers. Also included in the capsule were the names of the show's many fan club members, photos of the cast members, copies of the *Genoa City Chronicle,* and three books written about the show. The capsule is scheduled to be unearthed on the show's fiftieth anniversary, March 26, 2023.

During a pre–Daytime Emmy luncheon, seventy-one-year-old Bell announced that he was stepping down as the show's head writer "to catch his breath." He passed on the reins of head writer to Kay Alden, who had been working with him on the show since 1974.

1999: Y&R, which had been one of the first soap operas to incorporate images of its cast members in the opening credits, became the first to include the actors' real names under those images. A few months prior to that change, the names of the writers, directors, and producers were superimposed across both the show's opening and closing moments much as is done in primetime and feature films. This move was triggered by CBS's decision to reduce credit crawls to a nearly unreadable size to make room for more network promos. In addition to including the actor's real names, Y&R's revamped opening also jazzed up the theme music.

WHEN DID YOU GET HERE?

In the following puzzle, rearrange the following list of characters into the chronological order in which they were introduced on the show. Remember, it is the *character's* introduction that matters, not his or her current portrayer's. For an added challenge, see if you can remember in what year each character was introduced.

Christine Blair Williams	1. _____
Diane Jenkins Newman	2. _____
Jill Foster Abbott	3. _____
Katherine Chancellor	4. _____
Malcolm Winters	5. _____
Miguel Rodriguez	6. _____
Nina Webster McNeil	7. _____
Paul Williams	8. _____
Ryan McNeil	9. _____
Victor Newman	10. _____

Casting Stories

ALTHOUGH JEANNE Cooper has been playing Katherine Chancellor for twenty-six years and counting, she didn't want the role when executive producer John Conboy first approached her. Conboy, who had seen Cooper's work on film and television, was convinced that she would be perfect for the part, but she wasn't keen on joining a soap. Her poker pal K. T. Stevens (who had worked on *General Hospital* in its early days and would herself come on *Y&R* as Vanessa Prentiss) warned Cooper that soap work was boring. Taking Stevens's advice to heart, Cooper headed off to Hawaii with her family. Conboy refused to give up. He and Cooper's agent began calling each of the Hawaiian islands until they tracked her down. Cooper relented and agreed to play Katherine "for a little while."

Jaime Lyn Bauer had a choice to make in 1973: a seven-year contract with Universal Studios or a three-year contract to play Lorie Brooks on *The Young and the Restless.*

John McCook was not the first choice to play Lorie's crooning Romeo, Lance Prentiss. Another actor had actually been hired for the role. The actor was overwhelmed by the wardrobe fittings, the rehearsals, and the dual responsibility of not only acting but singing on camera. When he asked how many times a week he was expected to sing, the producers replied "almost every day." He quit on the spot. McCook was quickly recruited for the role. The day after his audition, he was on the set.

David Hasselhoff was a still a bit inexperienced when he auditioned to take over the role of Snapper Foster. When the director instructed him to move ten paces right to find his mark, Hasselhoff had no idea what the man was talking about. He looked around the set for another actor who might have been named Mark.

After Tom Ligon landed the role of Lucas Prentiss, the producers told him to shave off his beard. Although he was none too pleased with the request, his wife was thrilled. Eventually, he grew the beard back.

Several years ago, after watching a videotape of her screen test, Melody Thomas Scott (NIKKI REED) described her performance as "dreadful." When Y&R was looking to replace Erica Hope as Nikki Reed, the decision had come down to Thomas Scott or another actress, whom the producers considered prettier but less talented. When Thomas heard this through her agent, she couldn't decide whether to be complimented or insulted. At the same time, Thomas had been offered a role in a sitcom pilot. Although she preferred doing comedy, her agent convinced her to grab the sure thing, which turned out to be very good advice. The sitcom was never picked up.

Doug Davidson literally walked into his role of Paul Williams. He hadn't come to the studio to audition; he just stopped by to visit a friend, who was working on the show. While he was there, the producers spotted him, liked his look, and hired him.

When Michael Damian first performed on Dick Clark's American Bandstand, John Conboy happened to be watching. He subsequently offered Damian the role of rock star Danny Romalotti. Damian, who had never considered an acting career, took the role only because it would allow him to sing.

Producer H. Wesley Kenney had known Tracey E. Bregman (LAUREN FENMORE) from Days of Our Lives, where he had been a director and she played Donna Craig. One day, shortly after taking over the job as executive producer at Y&R, Kenney dropped by Bregman's house to see her father.

Kenney saw Bregman and told her that if she was ever interested in coming back to daytime, to let him know. Disappointed with the roles she was finding in primetime and feature films, Bregman took Kenney up on his offer.

Colleen Casey was performing a collection of standards by Cole Porter and George Gershwin at a nightclub where Bill Bell happened to stop by for a drink. As he listened to Casey sing, the character of Farren Connor developed in his head as a new love interest for Andy Richards (Steven Ford). Bell tracked Casey down and auditioned her for the role.

Thom Bierdz was called back for several auditions for the role of Phillip Chancellor, giving him time to study the show. He specifically scrutinized Phillip's less-than-devoted mother Jill, played by Brenda Dickson. By the time Bierdz came in for his screen test, he had worked up a strong dislike for Jill, which he took out on Dickson, treating her rudely and staring at her before, during, and after the screen test.

Because of the abrupt manner in which Brenda Dickson was fired from the role of Jill Abbott, her replacement, Jess Walton, was hired only eight hours before she was due on the set.

John Castellanos's brief turn as a lawyer on *The Bold and the Beautiful* served as his audition and screen test for Y&R. When the role of attorney John Silva came up, Bell asked specifically for Castellanos.

Few actors rebound from one soap to another quite as quickly or as successfully as Peter Bergman (JACK ABBOTT). All My Children fans and Bergman himself were shocked when he was fired in the fall of 1989. Luckily for Bergman, his firing occurred shortly after Terry Lester had decided to abandon the role of Jack Abbott on Y&R. Melody Thomas Scott (NIKKI NEWMAN) was familiar with Bergman's work on AMC and recommended that her husband, executive producer Ed Scott, audition him. Although Bergman has more than claimed the part as his own, he was not interested the first two times Y&R called his agent. He was winding down at AMC and didn't want to think about jumping right into another role. Debbi Morgan, who had been his last leading lady at *AMC*, told Bergman that he was crazy to turn down one of daytime's showcase roles. Furthermore, Bergman's wife was pregnant at the time, so he could not afford the luxury of turning work down. The day after Bergman taped his last scenes as Dr. Cliff Warner, he was flown in secrecy to Los Angeles. Less than two weeks after being fired by *All My Children*, Bergman was living on the other side of the country and starring on a higher rated soap.

There were only two daytime series on which J. Eddie Peck was interested in working: *All My Children* and *The Young and the Restless*. In 1993, both shows were interested in him as well. *Y&R* won out because the California-based Peck did not want to move his family across the country to New York, where *All My Children* is taped.

Leigh J. McCloskey (KURT COSTNER) had remained good friends with Ronn Moss (RIDGE FORRESTER, *The Bold and the Beautiful*) since they worked together on the 1989 Italian adventure film *Hearts and Armour*. When McCloskey was looking for work, Moss introduced him to Bill Bell. At the time, McCloskey had grown a beard and was wearing his hair down to his shoulders. That look inspired Bell to create the character of Kurt Costner, a mysterious drifter who turned out to be a doctor.

When Heather Tom vacated the role of Victoria Newman, a number of young actresses tried out for the highly coveted role, among them Sarah Aldrich, who landed the part, and Jennifer Gareis, who ended up replacing Josie Davis as Grace Turner shortly thereafter. On Gareis's first day of work, Aldrich spotted her in the make-up room. Recognizing Gareis from the Victoria audition, Aldrich worried that she was being replaced. Although she wasn't let go that day, her *Y&R* stint did end shortly thereafter when Heather Tom agreed to return.

When Nick Scotti announced he was leaving *Y&R*, Jay Bontatibus was one of several actors who auditioned to take over the role of Tony Viscardi. Bontatibus's audition tape, unfortunately, jammed in the casting director's VCR. While Bontatibus waited to hear from the show, his tape sat inside the machine in a repair shop. When the casting director got her VCR back and pressed the play button, she saw the remainder of Bontatibus's tape and realized that he would be perfect as Tony. A number of established soap opera names had been tossed about as possible replacement for Scotti, among them Ricky Paull Goldin (who now plays Gary Dawson) and George Palermo, who had once beaten Bontatibus out for the role of another Tony, Tony Soleito on *Loving*.

Before landing the role of Dr. Olivia Barber, Tonya Lee Williams recurred on the now defunct soap *Generations* as a girlfriend to Kristoff St. John's (NEIL WINTERS) character, Adam Marshall. Two weeks after she started on *Y&R*, *Generations* called to offer her a contract.

Shemar Moore (MALCOLM WINTERS) made a seamless transition from model to actor. Casting directors from *Y&R* spotted him in a small advertisement

Shemar Moore
was discovered
in *GQ*.
© *Albert Ortega,*
Moonglow Photos

in the men's fashion magazine *GQ* and realized that he would look right as Neil Winters's (Kristoff St. John) half-brother Malcolm. Ironically, Moore was not the first choice to appear in the GQ ad. He landed the job only after model/actor Jason Olive turned it down. Before Moore showed up for his *Y&R* audition, he spent eleven hours and eleven hundred dollars cramming with an acting coach.

Sandra Nelson was filming an episode of *Star Trek: Deep Space Nine* on the same day she was to screen test for the role of Phyllis Romalotti. *Star Trek* star LeVar Burton was directing the episode. As a fellow actor, he sympathized with her plight. He rearranged the schedule, allowing her to leave early. Even with the head start, Nelson's agent worried that she would miss the screen test as the make-up artists spent more than an hour and a half removing her Klingon face.

Because Veronica Landers would spend most of her screen time masquerading as a dowdy maid, Candice Daly was advised not to wear any make-up to the audition. She was, in fact, the only actress at the audition who didn't wear any.

David Lago was planning to sell his truck to make rent when he got the call that he'd landed the role of Raul.

A number of actors auditioned for one role and end up with another. Terry Lester, who originated the role of Jack Abbott, originally came to the attention of producer John Conboy when he tried out to fill William Grey Espy's shoes as Dr. Snapper Foster. Before taking on the role of evil nurse Sheila, Kimberlin Brown tried out for the role of Cassandra Rawlins, Paul Williams's mystery woman. Brown's onscreen rival, Tracey E. Bregman (Lauren Fenmore), originally tested to play Patty Williams, which would have cast her as Doug Davidson's (Paul Williams) sister instead of his lover. Amy Gibson was deemed too young to play the devious Lindsey Wells, but was hired the next year as mob princess Alana Anthony. Although producers thought Eddie Cibrian looked too old to play Nicholas Newman, his jock image helped him land the role of Nicholas's arch enemy Matt Clark, who was supposed to be about the same age.

1. On what World War II–based series did Eric Braeden (VICTOR NEWMAN) star as Captain Hans Dietrich?
(a) *Rat Patrol*
(c) *Combat*
(b) *Espionage*
(d) *McHale's Navy*

2. Which *Hogan's Heroes* regular played Pierre Roulland during *Y&R's* early years?
(a) Bob Crane
(c) Robert Clary
(b) Werner Klemperer
(d) Richard Dawson

3. In what two Westerns did Peter Brown (ROBERT LAURENCE) star in the 1950s and 1960s?
(a) *Wagon Train* and *The Westerner*
(c) *Rawhide* and *The Rifleman*
(b) *Bonanza* and *Big Valley*
(d) *Laredo* and *The Lawman*

4. What sitcom, based on a popular film, costarred both Tricia Cast (NINA WEBSTER MCNEIL) and Kristoff St. John (NEIL WINTERS)?
(a) *Fast Times at Ridgemont High*
(c) *9 to 5*
(b) *The Bad News Bears*
(d) *Dirty Dancing*

5. Which of the following actors never worked on the primetime serial *Dallas*?
(a) J. Eddie Peck (COLE HOWARD)
(c) Leigh McCloskey (KURT COSTNER)
(b) Marc Singer (CHET)
(d) Don Diamont (BRAD CARLTON)

6. Beverly Archer, who played Jill's maid Shirley Sherwood, costarred as eccentric next door neighbor Iola Boylen on what sitcom?
(a) *Mama's Family*
(c) *Coach*
(b) *Evening Shade*
(d) *Golden Girls*

7. On what early 1980s sci-fi series did Peter Barton (DR. SCOTT GRAINGER) play an extraterrestrial high school student?
   (a) *Alf*
   (b) *Battlestar Gallactica*
   (c) *The Powers of Matthew Star*
   (d) *The Bionic Woman*

8. With which caped hero did Michael Tylo (BLADE) battle on a weekly basis in the early 1990s?
   (a) Batman
   (b) Superman
   (c) The Shadow
   (d) Zorro

9. Josie Davis, who originated the role of Grace Turner, worked on what Scott Baio sitcom?
   (a) *Baby Talk*
   (b) *Joanie Loves Chachi*
   (c) *Charles in Charge*
   (d) *Who's Watching the Kids?*

10. Which actress played Urkel's girlfriend Myra on the sitcom *Family Matters?*
    (a) Victoria Rowell (DRUCILLA WINTERS)
    (b) Michelle Thomas (CALLIE ROGERS)
    (c) Wanda Acuna (KEESHA MONROE)
    (d) Tonya Lee Williams (DR. OLIVIA BARBER)

$\mathcal{M}issed\ Opportunities$

CAROLYN CONWELL (MARY WILLIAMS) had auditioned to play psychiatrist Marlena Evans on *Days of Our Lives*, the role that rocketed Y&R alumna Deidre Hall (BARBARA ANDERSON) to fame. Although the producers applauded Conwell's audition, she has stated that she was not given the role because she was not good-looking enough.

Bill Bell realized that the storyline in which Katherine Chancellor was kidnapped and replaced with a lookalike waitress opened up room for comedy. He wanted an older comic actor to play one of the criminals holding Katherine hostage. His first choice for the part was Mickey Rooney. After Rooney turned it down, Red Buttons was approached. Although Buttons had recently worked on the primetime soap *Knots Landing*, he wasn't interested. The part ultimately went to Morey Amsterdam, best known for his work on the 1960s sitcom *The Dick Van Dyke Show*.

Jeff Trachta, who would go on to play Thorne Forrester on *The Bold and the Beautiful*, was deemed too young to replace Terry Lester as Jack Abbott. Among the other actors who tried out for the role was Mark Pinter, who went on to become one of daytime's top schemers as *Another World's* Grant Harrison.

Peter Bergman, who did land the role of Jack Abbott, surprised many people by winning such a conniving part. Bergman, who had made a name for himself as *All My Children's* decent doctor Cliff Warner, had earlier tried out for the role of *One Life to Live*'s slimebag Brad Vernon, a role that went to Jameson Parker.

Peter Barton (DR. SCOTT GRAINGER) lost the role of *Guiding Light*'s angel Zachary to Brody Hutzler, who joined *Y&R* in 1999 as Cody.

Kurt Robin McKinney came close to landing the role of Dr. Scott Grainger back in 1988. Instead, that same year, he originated the role of Ned Ashton on *General Hospital,* a role that paired him with Sharon Case (SHARON NEWMAN). Since 1994, McKinney has been playing Matt Reardon on *Guiding Light.*

Joshua Morrow (NICHOLAS NEWMAN) originally tried out for the role of Dylan Shaw on *The Bold and the Beautiful.*

 J. Eddie Peck read for the role of *Santa Barbara*'s Connor McCabe, which went instead to Charles Grant (GRANT CHAMBERS, *The Bold and the Beautiful*). Peck, who realized that *Santa Barbara* was on its way out, did not put much passion into the audition.

Scott Reeves (Ryan McNeil) came close to landing the role of Brian Bodine on *All My Children.* The night before his screen test, he began to worry about what taking the part would mean to his marriage. His wife, Melissa, worked on the Los Angeles–based *Days of Our Lives.* Reeves was so upset at the prospect of a bicoastal marriage that he spent the night before the screen test throwing up. The next morning, he headed back to California and instructed his agent to pass on his regrets to ABC.

Among the actors who tried out for the role of Ryan McNeil was Steve Burton, who went on to win an Emmy as *General Hospital*'s amnesiac gangster Jason Morgan.

The choice for the lead female role in the John Hughes science-fiction/comedy film *Weird Science* came down to Kimberlin Brown (SHEILA CARTER) and Kelly LeBrock. LeBrock had the edge (and won the part) because she had played the title role in another successful comedy, *The Woman in Red.*

Days of Our Lives passed on Heather Tom.

© *Albert Ortega, Moonglow Photos*

Sabryn Genet (TRICIA DENNISON MCNEIL) and Sarah Aldrich (VICTORIA NEWMAN) shared a flight from Los Angeles to New York to compete against each other for the role of Kelsey Jefferson on *All My Children*.

Losing the role of Sarah Horton on *Days of Our Lives* turned out to be quite a blessing for Heather Tom. While Sarah Horton never enjoyed much of a storyline, Victoria Newman became one of the more prominent teenaged roles in daytime history.

David Tom (BILLY ABBOTT) lost out on the role of Pacey on the primetime series *Dawson's Creek* because he looked too much like James Van Der Beek, who had already been chosen as the lead.

Among the future movie stars whom *Y&R* passed over was Kevin Costner, who went on to achieve superstardom in films such as *Bull Durham* and *Dances with Wolves*.

If the Actors Had Their Way

TRACEY E. BREGMAN (LAUREN FENMORE), who suffers from claustrophobia, was horrified by the plot twist in which demented fan Shawn Garrett (Grant Cramer) buried her alive. Bregman explained her phobia to the producers, then asked for a stand-in for the scenes in which Lauren was buried. Unfortunately, the producers informed her, she was going to have to tough this scene out herself. Making the situation even more uncomfortable, time constraints prevented the crew from digging Bregman up for breaks.

Beth Maitland and her character Traci Abbott became role models for young women viewers due to Maitland's weight problem and Traci's socially conscious storylines—ranging from bulimia to diet pill addiction. As a result, Maitland was concerned about the storyline in which a distraught Traci attempted suicide. She worried about the message the suicide attempt would send to the many fans who looked up to Traci. Despite Maitland's objections, the storyline went forward as planned.

When the character of Ellen Winters was introduced, Jennifer Karr was as well dressed as any of the show's other leading ladies. She eventually convinced the producers that it would be more realistic for Ellen, who ran a soup kitchen, to dress a little more plainly.

Despite his leading-man good looks, Don Diamont (BRAD CARLTON) considers himself a comedian at heart. As such, he pestered the producers until they allowed him to work some humor into Brad and Traci's romance. In one scene, Brad cheered Traci up with his impression of the Three Stooges.

Although actors do not usually have a say in their dialogue, Victoria Rowell (DRUCILLA BARBER) and Shemar Moore (MALCOLM WINTERS) were once asked to spark up their lines with street lingo.

After Julianne Morris (AMY WILSON) read the script in which her character lost her virginity, she wrote a letter to Bill Bell expressing concern over the message that might be sent to the young viewers. Although many actors, especially newcomers like Morris, might have worried about upsetting the boss, the highly religious Morris felt strongly about the issue. Bell respected Morris's moral convictions and modified subsequent scripts to include the character's regret. Amy later referred to her one night stand with Nicholas Newman (Joshua Morrow) as "the worst decision of my life."

When Melody Thomas Scott learned that Nikki was to become involved with her gynecologist, she half-jokingly begged that Dr. Landers (Heath Kizzier) be given a different specialty.

Some of the newer cast members laughed when they read that Jabot's new line of teen cosmetics was to be named Brash'n Sassy. In a mood to impress his younger colleagues, Kristoff St. John (NEIL WINTERS) picked up the studio phone and called Bill Bell's office. When Bell answered, St. John explained that he and some of the other actors on the show were having a hard time taking the name Brash'n Sassy seriously. Bell informed St. John that he should concentrate on his acting and leave such creative decisions as naming the cosmetics to the writers. A contrite St. John apologized and hung up the phone.

On Their Way Out

IN THE mid-1970s, Janice Lynde (LESLIE BROOKS) was involved in a rather serious car accident, in which she injured her neck and back. The show's producers were not willing to grant her sufficient time off to properly recover. Instead, she reported for work medicated on painkillers. The way that she was treated during this period led to her decision not to re-sign with the show when her contract expired. Both physically and emotionally exhausted, she chose to take time off from acting.

William Grey Espy left the role of Dr. Snapper Foster in 1975 in order to travel to remote parts of the world, such as New Zealand, India, and Nepal. During his absence from daytime television, a rumor circulated that he had joined a monastery.

Brenda Dickson got married in 1973, the same year that she originated the role of schemer extraordinaire Jill Foster. In 1980, she left the show to devote herself to becoming a stay-at-home wife. When the marriage dissolved three years later, Dickson returned to the show.

Jim McMullan was replaced by Bert Kramer in the role of Brent Davis, Ashley Abbott's (Eileen Davidson) biological father, because the producers decided that they wanted the character to be a little grittier.

Amy Gibson (ALANA ANTHONY) had been warned four times to control her weight problem. Comments about her weight and pressure from the producers to shed pounds pushed a resentful Gibson to overeat. Eventually, she was dismissed from the show because of her weight.

As Mari Jo Mason's mental health began to deteriorate, her portrayer, Diana Barton, saw the writing on the wall. She went to coordinating producer Nancy Wiard's office to ask directly if Mari Jo was being written off the show. Coincidentally, the writers and producers were discussing that very same issue when Barton showed up.

Joshua Morrow (NICHOLAS NEWMAN) had been seriously considering leaving the show when he broke his leg playing basketball. The time he spent recuperating gave him the opportunity to reflect upon his career goals. He was also moved by the producers' decision not to bring in another actor to replace him while he recovered. Impressed by this show of loyalty, Morrow decided to stay on.

Backstage Pass

MEMBERS OF the press are rarely invited onto the set of *The Young and the Restless,* but stories leak out about what it's like behind the scenes. Although *Y&R* is one of the best looking shows on daytime, it has had its share of accidents, flubbed lines, and practical jokes.

PROFESSIONAL COURTESY

Because *Y&R* creator/writer/producer Bill Bell knew that his presence on the set made his daughter Lauralee (Christine "Cricket" Blair) nervous, he made a point of never visiting the set while she was taping or rehearsing her scenes.

Peter Bergman prides himself on his punctuality. Since taking over the role of Jack Abbott in 1989, he has never been late for work.

When Heather Tom (VICTORIA NEWMAN) was a teenager she noticed that crew members would clean up their language when she walked onto the set.

DRESSING ROOMS

Because Jeanne Cooper (KATHERINE CHANCELLOR) considers "every day a gift," she keeps a Christmas tree in her dressing room all year. Each year she adds an ornament to the tree lifted from one of the set's Christmas trees.

Jess Walton (JILL FOSTER ABBOTT) often spends her lunch hour playing chess in her dressing room with a prop manager from *The Bold and the Beautiful.*

Melody Thomas Scott (NIKKI NEWMAN) has the same dressing room that Cher used while starring on *The Sonny and Cher Show* back in the 1970s. When Thomas Scott first took over the dressing room, it was decorated with a Native American motif.

During a trip to New York for the Daytime Emmys, Peter Bergman (JACK ABBOTT) and his wife, Mariellen, passed by the location where *All My Children* was once taped. (For ten years, Bergman had played Dr. Cliff Warner on the show.) The building that housed the *AMC* studio had been leveled, a fact that hit Bergman harder than he imagined it would. After Bergman and his wife went their separate ways for the day, Mariellen snuck back to the site and grabbed one of the bricks from the old studio, which were lying on the ground. The brick now sits in Bergman's dressing room at *Y&R*.

TRICKS OF THE TRADE

Eric Braeden (VICTOR NEWMAN) underwent root canal right before Victor was to share a romantic dinner with Nikki (Melody Thomas Scott). The cameramen compensated for Braeden's swollen face by shooting him only from his good side. Observant viewers may have also picked up on the fact that Nikki was the only one who ate during the entire scene.

Alex Donnelley was nearly eight months pregnant during a scene in which Diane tried to seduce Andy Richards (Steven Ford). Because the character was not supposed to be pregnant, her stomach was concealed behind a well-placed cowboy hat.

Whenever Michael Damian (DANNY ROMALOTTI) or Beth Maitland (TRACI ABBOTT) discovered a song they wanted to perform on the show, they usually had a difficult time pinning Bill Bell down long enough for him to give it a listen. When Bell's daughter Lauralee still lived with her parents, she took advantage of that fact to help her friends out. After Bill Bell settled into his chair at home, Lauralee would pop a cassette into the tape deck and convince her father that they should use the song on the show.

Whenever Tonya Lee Williams (Dr. OLIVIA BARBER) knows that she has a major crying scene coming up, she cuts back significantly on her salt intake, as she knows salt causes her to retain water.

After being shot by his wife, Nina (Tricia Cast), David Kimble (Michael Corbett) faked being catatonic. To pull off his charade, David had to stare straight forward for weeks on end, never letting his eyes blink, a challenge Corbett once described as "a bear."

Long before David Kimble faked his catatonic state, Cathy Carricaburu played Nancy Becker's catatonia for nearly a year. Because Nancy wasn't allowed to blink, Carricaburu always removed her contact lenses before each scene began.

Backstage prankster Scott Reeves.
© Sue Schneider, Moonglow Photos

Signy Coleman, who played the blind Hope Newman, found it most effective to focus her attention on a point just to the side of the person with whom she was engaged in dialogue. She then concentrated on listening to the words rather than looking at the actor directly.

PRACTICAL JOKES

In the 1980s, when Alex Donnelley's storyline involved her with Doug Davidson (PAUL WILLIAMS) and Steven Ford (ANDY RICHARDS), she earned a reputation as a practical joker. After meeting comic actor Leslie Nielsen (*The Naked Gun*) at a fundraiser, she picked up his game of playing with noisemakers. The noisemakers were loud enough for Davidson and Ford but not the sound men or boom operators to hear. Eventually, one of the producers took Donnelley's toys away from her.

One scene called for Ryan McNeil (Scott Reeves) to break up a fight between brothers Malcolm and Neil Winters (Shemar Moore and Kristoff St. John). Right before he jumped into the mix, Reeves pulled off his shirt, revealing a T-shirt decorated with a Superman-style "S."

Signy Coleman (HOPE ADAMS NEWMAN) plotted with the make-up artist to pull a joke on her onscreen husband Eric Braeden (VICTOR NEWMAN). Whenever the taping started to drag, Braeden was famous for his remark, "Let's shoot this." As he was standing on the set one day, Hayden Tank, who played Victor's young son, walked out, his face made up with a Victor Sr. mustache, and announced, "Let's shoot this." Even though he was the target of the joke, Braeden couldn't help laughing.

Throughout Drucilla's (Victoria Rowell) pregnancy, she worried that the baby could be her brother-in-law Malcolm's (Shemar Moore) child and not her husband Neil's. After she delivered the child, someone drew Moore's trademark goatee onto the doll Rowell would be cuddling in her scenes.

During the scene in which Nina (Tricia Cast) lay comatose in her hospital bed, her onscreen husband, Scott Reeves, poured a pitcher of water over her head just for fun. Cast got her revenge after taping a subsequent scene—she pulled out a cream pie from underneath the bedcovers and smacked him right in the face.

WARDROBE

The 1984 wedding between Nikki Reed (Melody Thomas) and Victor Newman (Eric Braeden) required a spectacular gown. The one Thomas wore took fifteen weeks and a total of five hundred hours to produce. Much of that time was taken up applying some twenty thousand beads and pearls. The price tag for the wedding dress was twenty-five thousand dollars. Underneath the expensive gown, Scott as Nikki wore a pair of men's polka dot boxer shorts.

When filming love scenes, J. Eddie Peck (COLE HOWARD) prefers to wear two pairs of underwear.

During certain love scenes, the bed sheet would literally be pinned to Brenda Dickson's (JILL FOSTER ABBOTT) bodysuit.

Although Tracey E. Bregman's second pregnancy was incorporated into Lauren Fenmore's storyline, Bregman herself did not look exceptionally pregnant. She gained so little weight that the producers decided to pad her the same way they would have done with a non-pregnant actress.

When Paul posed nude while Lauren took pictures, Doug Davidson wore a flesh-colored pair of cover-ups. Although he was not really exposed, some fans with good imagination insist that they saw more than they actually did.

HAIR . . .

Brenda Dickson's (JILL FOSTER ABBOTT) hair went through a number of changes in length, style, and color over the years. At times, Dickson would change her hair color in the middle of an exceptionally long scene. If a scene were to run over the course of several taping days, the producers could never guarantee that Jill's hair would remain the same from one day to the next. Executive producer John Conboy always suspected that something was brewing when Dickson came down to rehearsals with a towel wrapped around her head. Dickson usually kept her changes secret until the cameras were set to roll.

When Nina Arvesen was hired to play Paul Williams's (Doug Davidson) new mystery woman, Cassandra Rawlins, there were quite a few prominent blondes already in the cast. Arvesen was therefore instructed to dye her hair a darker color. After a number of those blonde actresses left the show, she was allowed to go back to her natural color.

During the 1980s, Brett Hadley would be called in to play Carl Williams whenever the script had a need for him. On one such occasion, Hadley shocked the producers by showing up at the studio completely bald. He had shaved his head for the heck of it in between his *Y&R* stints. Hadley was then outfitted with a wig.

. . . AND MAKE-UP

During Katherine Chancellor's jungle adventure, the character's leg became badly infected. The make-up artist did such a remarkable and realistic job creating a sore on Jeanne Cooper's leg that the actress literally gagged when Katherine removed her bandage for the first time.

Sharon Case's (SHARON NEWMAN) mother was so impressed with the way her daughter's make-up looked onscreen that she would occasionally ask Case for beauty tips. Case reminded her mother that the make-up is applied by professionals, not by herself.

When coming up with the "Sarah" disguise for Candice Daly's character Veronica, the make-up artists experimented with—and rejected—the idea of putting baby bottle nipples up her nose to make her nostrils flare.

The look the make-up artists came up with for Daly—a mousy brown wig and pockmarked face—was certainly eye catching. While in make-up, Daly would often refrain from heading down to the commissary for lunch because she was tired of the stares she received and the comments she overheard about how pretty she might have been if she tried.

Remembering Their Lines

Andrea Evans (PATTY ABBOTT) never had much trouble remembering her lines, as she has been blessed with a photographic memory.

Peter Bergman (JACK ABBOTT) is very studious about learning his lines because he doesn't like to use cue cards. He likes to get lost in the role, and cue cards remind him that he's not Jack Abbott.

A scene from the early 1980s had Paul Williams (Doug Davidson) escorting Katherine Chancellor (Jeanne Cooper) home. As Paul helped Katherine off with her coat, he was supposed to mention that his father was a police officer. Mixing up his dialogue with his stage direction, Paul removed Katherine's jacket and said, "Well, Mrs. Chancellor, my dad's a coat."

In a pivotal scene between Katherine and Jill (Brenda Dickson), Jill was supposed to tell Katherine that she was pregnant with her husband Phillip's child. Dickson simply could not get the line out—despite Cooper's varied promptings. At first, Cooper ad-libbed a question, asking if Jill was feeling all right. When that didn't trigger Dickson's memory, Cooper gave a more direct hint. "Are you sick to your stomach?" she asked. Again, nothing. Finally, an exasperated Cooper asked, "Did you come here to tell me that you're pregnant with my husband's child?"

Accidents Will Happen

Ken Olandt and Lauralee Bell got a little physical during the scene in which Derek Stuart raped Cricket Blair. For the first week of filming after that scene, the make-up department did not need to apply any fake bruises to Bell's arms. Olandt had held her so tightly during the scene that he'd left an imprint of his thumb and all four fingers on one of her arms.

Wings Hauser (GREG FOSTER) occasionally fasted to drop some extra pounds. One time, he became lightheaded due to the lack of food and he had to stop the tape during a scene.

Jill Abbott (Jess Walton) and Leanna Love's (Barbara Crampton) competition for Michael Crawford (Colby Chester) erupted into a nasty restaurant confrontation that ended with Jill throwing a glass of water into Leanna's face. Unfortunately for Crampton, the scene needed to be taped several times. Walton's acting was on target during the scene, but her aim wasn't. Water splashed Crampton in the chin and against her blouse. She was soaked by the time Walton landed one glass of water square in her face.

While filming a scene in which Matt Miller rescued Ashley Abbott (Eileen Davidson) from a fire, Robert Parucha ripped his pants. Because the camera was going to be doing only close-ups of his face and upper body, the wardrobe staff did not bother to repair the pants or find the actor another pair. At one point during the scene, Parucha bent down the wrong way, giving the camera a perfect view of the split. The image was edited out of the final scene.

During a fight scene with his onscreen brother, Neil (Kristoff St. John), Shemar Moore (MALCOLM WINTERS) tripped and slammed his head against the fireplace set. The gaffe looked so good that the producers decided to leave it in when the show aired.

One hospital scene called for Jack Abbott (Peter Bergman) to come rushing in after his then-wife Nikki (Melody Thomas Scott) had fallen down the stairs drunk. As Bergman hurried through the hospital set, he hit a cable on the ground and slid nearly twenty feet down the corridor.

Sunset Beach's Hank Cheyne played the minor role of Lauren Fenmore's (Tracey E. Bregman) keyboardist in the mid-1980s. When Lauren's obsessed manager Shawn Garrett (Grant Cramer) suspected that Lauren was interested in Cheyne's character, he blew him up along with his keyboard. The explosion was done in one take, which was all they had been given to get it right. Cheyne had not been nervous about the explosion until he noticed that the show's regulars were uneasy and the cameraman was shielded by a sheet of Plexiglas.

When Millie (Ernestine Mercer) decided to let her granddaughter Cassie (Camryn Grimes) leave with Tony and Grace (Nick Scotti and Jennifer Gareis), she sent the young girl upstairs to pack. The way the sets are constructed, the staircases don't actually lead anywhere. So Grimes walked to the top and waited for someone to tell her that she could come back down. The crew, however, forgot that she was up there and started to shut down the set. When they turned off the lights, Grimes called down to remind them of her presence.

TEMPTING THE CENSORS

One of Michelle Stafford's sex scenes as Phyllis Romalotti was supposed to end with her walking away from the bed. The audience was supposed to see merely her bare back. Stafford, however, wanted to give the moment something more. At the last moment, she turned to face the camera, covering her breasts with her hands. CBS asked the show to reshoot the scene as originally planned.

Even after Sandra Nelson took over the role of Phyllis, the character remained one of the show's most provocative characters. One sex scene between her and sleazy lawyer Michael Baldwin (Christian LeBlanc) found Phyllis dressed in dominatrix boots and leather while holding a riding crop. Michael wore handcuffs. The producers also shot a tamer version of the scene, in case the censors objected.

Joshua Morrow (NICHOLAS NEWMAN) was amazed that a scene in which Nicholas licked Sharon's (Sharon Case) stomach made it onto the airwaves.

Postcards from the Road

IN 1984, Nikki Reed (Melody Thomas Scott) headed to the island of St. Croix with her homicidal boyfriend Rick Daros (Randy Holland), who plotted to murder her during a scuba diving adventure. Although almost every other soap opera was filming remotes around the world, including St. Croix, Y&R ventured no further than Palos Verdes, California, for the beachside scenes.

The finale to the Brad Carlton (Don Diamont) kidnapping story sent Tracey E. Bregman (LAUREN FENMORE) and Terry Lester (JACK ABBOTT) to Lake Tahoe. While on a ski trip, Lauren and Jack happened upon the cabin where Brad's ex-wife was keeping him caged. Although Bregman loves to ski, she refrained from taking to the slopes during the excursion except as called for in the script. She was afraid of hurting herself and throwing the remote off schedule.

A number of cast members headed to Hawaii for the long-awaited wedding of Christine Blair (Lauralee Bell) and Danny Romalotti (Michael Damian). Director Nancy Wiard, who had her share of weather problems on previous location shoots, took out an extra insurance policy for the wedding. Before taping began, Wiard asked a kahuna (a Hawaiian priest) to bless the shoot. As Wiard hoped, weather conditions for the shoot could not have been better.

The producers brought the cameras back to Hawaii four years later. This time, Hawaii substituted for Vietnam as Christine and Paul Williams went searching for the son Jack Abbott had fathered while fighting in the war.

The scene in which Phyllis Romalotti (Michelle Stafford) ran down Paul (Doug Davidson) and Christine on their would-be wedding day took the crew to Pittsburgh, Pennsylvania. During the shoot, the temperature dropped to freezing. Davidson, who had been born and raised in California, experienced a first—he had never before seen sleet.

When Drucilla Barber (Victoria Rowell) and Neil Winters (Kristoff St. John) married, the producers originally planned to tape their honeymoon in the studio. The script had not yet specified exactly where Neil and Dru were headed; it was only known that they were going somewhere with a beach. Rowell and St. John, who were scheduled to travel to the

Kristoff St. John and Victoria Rowell turned a personal appearance into an onscreen honeymoon.

© *Albert Ortega, Moonglow Photos*

Caribbean island of Antigua for a personal appearance, suggested to executive producer Ed Scott that they could film some scenes while they were there.

Paul and Christine's honeymoon took Doug Davidson and Lauralee Bell to the island of Nevis, just two miles south of St. Kitts. Bell, who is afraid of flying, found the twelve-hour flight a little taxing on her nerves—especially because they had to get on a small plane to hop over to another island for some of the remote's beach scenes. One of the more memorable highlights of the storyline found Christine's arch enemy, Phyllis Romalotti (Michelle Stafford), placing a dead octopus in Paul and Christine's bed. In real life, however, it was an animal of a different sort that vexed Bell. While shooting one horseback riding scene, Bell fell off her mount. The horse turned around and charged her. Its hooves missed her by less than an inch. Rather than reshoot using a different horse, the producers decided to scrap the scene altogether.

Bell and Davidson traveled back to Pittsburgh for the airport scene in which Chris and Paul prevent Grace (Jennifer Gareis) from running off with Cassie (Camryn Grimes). The shoot prevented Bell from spending her first married Valentine's Day with her new husband.

Last-Minute Changes

THE CHARACTER of Victor Newman (Eric Braeden) was introduced in 1980 with the intention of being killed off three months down the line. Bill Bell, however, was not pleased with the recast of Lance Prentiss—Dennis Cole had taken over from John McCook—or with the prospect of losing David Hasselhoff (DR. SNAPPER FOSTER) to primetime. Feeling that the show needed another strong male presence, Bell reconsidered Victor's death.

J. Eddie Peck's strong resemblance to Eric Braeden helped him land the role of Victor Newman's son, Cole Howard. When Cole met Victoria Newman (Heather Tom), Peck added a flirtatious smile to the scene. The producers cautioned Peck that Cole was smiling that way at his own sister, to which Peck replied that Cole was unaware of the connection. Because none of the actors being considered as Victoria's new love interest shared the same chemistry with Tom that Peck did, the producers abandoned the long-lost son storyline in favor of a Cole/Victoria romance. After a few months of dancing around the incest issue, the writers back-pedaled to reveal that Cole was not Victor's son after all.

The character of Douglas Austin was originally conceived as a Southern con artist. The producers were quite taken, however, with British-born Michael Evans's audition. After he was cast, Douglas was changed from a Southerner to a Brit.

When Jill Abbott (Brenda Dickson) was gunned down in her shower, the writers originally envisioned her being shot in the chest. The show's medical consultant advised them that the chance of her recovering from such a wound was extremely remote. By airtime, her would-be killer aimed his gun at her abdomen.

The George Rawlins murder mystery, as first conceived by the writers, would have ended with Paul Williams (Doug Davidson) learning that his lover, George's widow, Cassandra (Nina Arvesen), was the killer. Something about Arvesen, however, appealed to the writers, who decided to keep her around. Shortly into the storyline, before her guilt had been written in stone, the writers introduced the character of Adrian Hunter (Mark Derwin), a hitman whom the dying George Rawlins had paid to kill him and frame Paul.

When the wardrobe department first learned of the 1991 masquerade ball that would wrap up the David Kimble (Michael Corbett) story, costume suggestions were assigned to each character. The wardrobers, for example, wanted to dress Danny Romalotti (Michael Damian) up as Elvis Presley. Not only would the costume have fit with Danny's rock-and-roll persona, it would also have complemented his wife Christine's (Lauralee Bell) Marilyn Monroe outfit. For storyline reasons, however, the Elvis costume was vetoed. The writers needed Danny dressed in something that would hide his face so that David Kimble could masquerade as Danny. Ultimately, Danny attended the ball as the Big Bad Wolf.

Shemar Moore's Malcolm Winters was far more of a ladies' man when the character was first introduced. Some viewers regard his sexual encounter with his sister-in-law, Drucilla (Victoria Rowell), while she was high on flu medicine as nothing short of rape. When Drucilla subsequently learned that she was pregnant, she didn't know who the baby's father was. By this time, the audience was responding so positively to Shemar Moore that Bill Bell regretted the borderline rape. Although Bell could not change what viewers had seen, he has chosen to ignore it. He told *TV Guide*'s Michael Logan that he never pursued the paternity storyline because it could have destroyed the character of Malcolm, who has since been re-envisioned as a good guy.

At one point, the writers planned to bring on a brother for Brad Carlton (Don Diamont). Patrick Muldoon, who later starred on *Days of Our Lives* and *Melrose Place,* auditioned for the role, but ultimately the idea was abandoned.

When Barbara Crampton first began as Leanna Randolph, the character was more than a little quirky. Obsessed with her old psychiatrist, Steven Lassiter (Rod Arrants), she tried to kill his new bride, Ashley Abbott (Eileen Davidson). Along the way, Bill Bell recognized Crampton's flair for comedy and toned down the character's homicidal tendencies.

During the storyline in which Danny Romalotti (Michael Damian) landed the lead role in *Joseph and the Amazing Technicolor Dreamcoat,* the musical's producer, Andrew Lloyd Webber, was supposed to make a guest appearance as himself. At the last minute, however, shyness got the better of him.

GENOA CITY'S TEN MOST WANTED LIST

In the following puzzle, identify the villains by their signature crimes.

1. _____ sold Nina Webster's (Tricia Cast) first child on the black market.

2. _____ shot Jill Abbott (Brenda Dickson) in the shower.

3. _____ tried to murder Ashley Abbott (Eileen Davidson) with a poisoned lei.

4. _____ buried Lauren Fenmore (Tracey E. Bregman) alive.

5. _____ raped Sharon Collins (Sharon Case) and Amy Wilson (Julianne Morris).

6. _____ caged Brad Carlton (Don Diamont) in her family's cabin.

7. _____ married Flo Webster (Sharon Farrell), then plotted to murder her rich daughter Nina.

8. _____ replaced Lauren Fenmore's newborn son with a black-market baby.

9. _____ ran the mob in Genoa City.

10. _____ posed as Nikki's (Melody Thomas Scott) maid before gunning down Nikki and her husband, Josh.

The Line Between Fact and Fiction

FEW ACTORS' storylines have paralleled their real lives as closely as Jeanne Cooper's. From the time Cooper debuted on the show, Katherine Chancellor suffered from a drinking problem and ultimately joined Alcoholics Anonymous. Years later, Cooper developed a drinking problem of her own, a problem she has openly discussed in magazines and on talk shows.

In the mid-1980s, when Cooper decided that she wanted to have a facelift, a facelift was not only written into Katherine's storyline, film footage from Cooper's own operation was used on the show—the ultimate merger of fact and fiction.

Years later, when Cooper decided that the time had come for a touch up, both she and Katherine headed back to the hospital for a chemical peel. That procedure, however, did not make it to the air. Viewers did not see Katherine until after her face had healed, because the chemical peel was considered too unpleasant a process to watch.

Most recently, Cooper has been helping her divorced son Collin raise his two children. Cooper considered the phenomenon of grandparents raising their grandchildren worthy of exploring on the show. In the spring of 1999, she got her wish. The show introduced the character of Mackenzie (Ashley Bashioum), a teenaged granddaughter Katherine had never known. Mackenzie, whose father, Brock, had been presumed killed overseas, moved into the Chancellor mansion with Katherine.

Katherine and her fourth husband, Rex Sterling (Quinn Redeker), divorced in 1990. Two years later, they remarried. Redeker himself had divorced his first wife in the mid-1960s only to remarry her a year later.

In 1986, singer Lauren Fenmore (Tracey E. Bregman) was stalked by Shawn Garrett (Grant Cramer), a psychotic fan who ultimately buried her alive. Bregman was so unnerved by the psycho fan storyline that she started turning down public appearances. It took her a while to get over the feeling of vulnerability.

When Bregman was pregnant with her first child, a pregnancy storyline was created for Lauren as well. Unfortunately, Bregman miscarried, and shortly thereafter, Lauren did as well. Bill Bell offered to hire another actress to play the miscarriage scenes, but Bregman felt that she needed to do them herself. What she didn't want was for Bell to incorporate her subsequent pregnancy into Lauren's storyline—but he did. He contrived a storyline in which Lauren's arch rival Sheila Carter (Kimberlin Brown) kidnapped Lauren's newborn and replaced it with an infant who subsequently died. Looking back on that storyline—one of Lauren's most powerful and popular— Bregman is glad that Bell did not honor her request.

In the late '80s, Roberta Leighton, who plays Dr. Casey Reed, passed a real-life medical crisis with flying colors. While she was dining out in Beverly Hills, another customer suffered a heart attack. Leighton saved his life by administering CPR and keeping him calm until the paramedics arrived.

John Gibson was more than prepared to take on the role of Jerry "Cash" Cashman, a male stripper who performed at the Bayou Club along with Nikki Reed (Melody Thomas Scott). Before getting into acting, he made his living as a Chippendale dancer.

Peter Barton, who played Dr. Scott Grainger, originally intended to become a doctor. He began modeling and acting as a way to pay for medical school.

Brody Hutzler, whose character Cody works at Crimson Lights, knows his way around a coffee house—he used to work at Starbucks. Among his regular customers was *Guiding Light's* Kim Zimmer.

On *Y&R*, when Nicholas Newman was a baby, he swallowed a dime and required infant CPR. A few days after Melody Thomas Scott, who plays Nicholas's mother Nikki, taped the scene, her own seven-month-old daughter, Elizabeth, choked on a piece of food and required a similar procedure.

Michael Damian took on the role of rock star Danny Romalotti because it allowed him the opportunity to sing as well as act. Damian's musical talents were showcased in rehearsal scenes as well as concerts, occasionally encompassing an entire episode. The line between fiction and reality intercepted in 1989 when Damian's single "Rock On" hit the top of the pop charts. On the show, it was Danny Romalotti who had released the single.

When Michael Damian landed the lead role in the Los Angeles production of *Joseph and the Amazing Technicolor Dreamcoat*, the show worked around his schedule by writing the production into Danny's storyline. Like Damian, Danny landed the role of Joseph. *Y&R* fans saw Danny—and in turn Michael—practicing for the show. On the show, the production's heavy rehearsal and performance schedule created a rift between Danny and his wife Christine (Lauralee Bell). When *Joseph* moved from California to Broadway, Damian needed an extended leave of absence. Again fiction mirrored real life as Danny headed to New York with the play.

The Game of the Name

EARLY IN the show's history, creators Bill and Lee Phillip Bell named several of the characters after their own children. Bill Foster Jr. (William Grey Espy, David Hasselhoff) was named after Bill Bell Jr. Of course, few people ever called Bill Foster by his given name; he was better known as Snapper. At one point, Snapper's long lost father, William Foster (Charles Gray), returned to town, giving the show's creator an onscreen namesake.

Two characters were named after Bill Bell's son, Bradley, now head writer for *The Bold and the Beautiful*—Dr. Brad Eliot (Tom Hallick), who appeared during the show's early years, and Bradley Carlton (Don Diamont), who recently returned to town. Lauralee Brooks (Jaime Lyn Bauer), Lorie for short, was named after Bell's daughter, Lauralee, who now plays Christine Williams. Although there has yet to be a major character named Lee (as in Lee Phillip Bell), there have been three generations of Phillip Chancellors. Traci and Brad's daughter, who will more than likely pop up in Genoa City as a teen one day, was named Colleen after Bradley Bell's wife.

Victor Newman's (Eric Braeden) search for his biological mother led him to Cora Miller (Dorothy McGuire) and the revelation that Victor had been born with the name Christian. Christian happens to be the first name of Braeden's own son.

Although many viewers believe that Victoria Newman (Heather Tom) was named after her father, Victor (Eric Braeden), she was technically named

Lauralee Bell and her onscreen namesake
Lauralee Brooks (Jaime Lyn Bauer).

© *Albert Ortega, Moonglow Photos*

after Kevin Bancroft's (Christopher Holder) grandmother. When Victoria was born, Nikki was married to Kevin.

For the first two years that Doug Davidson was on the show, his character, Paul, was not given a last name. When the writers decided to build a family around Paul, a last name became imperative. Paul was given the last name Williams, which gave the character the same name as singer–songwriter–actor Paul Williams, who co-wrote the Barbra Streisand hit "Evergreen." When the real Paul Williams joined the cast of *The Bold and the Beautiful*, he made a point of meeting his Genoa City namesake.

In 1980, Doug Davidson met his future wife Cindy Fisher when she played a cult member named Rebecca. Two years later, his character fell in love with a hooker named Cindy.

Nathan Purdee so impressed the show with his performance as a mob enforcer known simply as Kong that the writers decided to expand upon the role. As part of that expansion, he was given a whole name, Nathan Hastings, named after Purdee himself.

Phyllis Romalotti (Michelle Stafford), one of the show's sexiest vixens, was named after Phyllis Diller, who shot to fame as a comedienne known for cracking jokes about her unattractive appearance. Diller had known Bill and Lee Phillip Bell since their earlier days living in Chicago.

Christopher Templeton (Carol Robbins) was named after Christopher Robin, the young boy in A. A. Milne's *Winnie the Pooh* stories. Not coincidentally, her character's last name was derived from the fictional boy's last name.

Rose, the black-market baby peddler played by Darlene Conley, was given the appropriately villainous last name DeVille, inspired by puppy-snatcher Cruella de Vil in the Disney classic *101 Dalmatians*.

Because Heath Kizzier's character was named Joshua Landers, he occasionally wound up with a script intended for Joshua Morrow, who plays

Nicholas Newman, and vice versa. There was also a similar mix-up with Morrow getting scripts meant for Nick Scotti, who played Tony Viscardi.

Although relatively new to the show, Nina Arvesen (CASSANDRA RAWLINS) was asked to present an award to Broadcast Marketing Executives. When she arrived at the ceremony, a number of people commented upon how different she looked in person. She soon realized that everyone had been expecting Tricia Cast, who played Nina on the show.

Tricia Cast herself was a little unnerved when she learned that the other woman to whom Nina would lose her husband Ryan (Scott Reeves) would also be named Tricia (Sabryn Genet).

When Brett Hadley returned to the show in the late 1990s as the long missing Carl Williams, it was revealed that Carl was suffering from amnesia and believed his name to be Jim Bradley. Bradley, it should be noted, is a combination of Hadley's first and last names: Br[ett] + [H]adley.

John Castellanos, who has played John Silva for the past decade, found most of the names the writers suggested for his character too ethnic. As time began running out, the name John was tagged onto the character. Because the character was initially conceived as short-term, the writers did not worry that there was already a prominent John—John Abbott (Jerry Douglas), as well as a Jack (Terry Lester)—among the cast of characters. As Castellanos's character caught on, the show found itself with two characters with the same first name—a rarity on daytime. Ironically, the two Johns and Jack have all been involved with Jill Abbott (Jess Walton) both in romance and business.

The Artists Formerly Known As . . .

AFTER COMING to the United States from Germany, Eric Braeden (VICTOR NEWMAN) worked in film and television under his given name, Hans Gudegast. For the most part, Braeden was relegated to playing Nazis in World War II dramas, such as the 1960s TV series *The Rat Patrol*. Because of a lingering anti-German sentiment, Braeden was advised that the name Hans Gudegast would severely limit his acting opportunities. Although he agreed to find a name more acceptable to the American public, he made sure to choose one connected to his German roots. Eric had been a popular name in his family; Braeden he took from the town in Germany where he grew up. Around his own home, though, Braeden is still called Hans.

After leaving *The Young and the Restless*, Thom Bierdz (PHILLIP CHANCELLOR III) radically altered his name as a privacy issue for his family. Although he has worked little in the decade after his character was killed off, he uses the professional name Zoey Drake.

K. T. Stevens (VANESSA PRENTISS) has gone by a number of names during the varied stages in her career. As a child actress, she went by Gloria Wood, her given name. When she later broke into movies as an adult, she'd taken on the screen name Katherine Stevens. By the time she reached *Young and the Restless*, she had shortened Katherine to the initials K. T.

Like Stevens, Wings Hauser, who played Greg Foster, has also gone by a variety of names during his career. Born Gerald Dwight Hauser, he has gone by the initials J. D. and the first name Ken before settling on his distinctive moniker.

Robert Clary (PIERRE ROULLAND) was born Robert Max Wiederman.

Both of the show's John Abbotts have changed their names. Brett Halsey, who originated the role, was born Charles Oliver Hand. He has also gone by the name Montgomery Ford. Jerry Douglas, who replaced Halsey as John, was born Gerald Rubenstein.

Lynne Topping (CHRIS BROOKS FOSTER) became Lynne Richter after getting married.

Tracey E. Bregman's (LAUREN FENMORE) name has changed a few times over the years. She started out as Tracey Bregman but added her middle initial upon the advice of a numerologist. When she married real estate developer Ron Recht, she became Tracey Bregman Recht. (She once joked that

Tracey E. Bregman aka Tracey Bregman Recht.
© *Albert Ortega, Moonglow Photos*

she didn't want to be known as Tracey E. Recht.) During a troubled period in that marriage, she reverted to Tracey E. Bregman. Although she and her husband have reconciled, she has stuck with Tracey E. Bregman.

Like Bregman, a number of her female cast mates have added their husband's surnames only to drop them later. When Veronica Redd (MAMIE JOHNSON) returned to Y&R after her divorce, she had abandoned the hyphenate -Forrest. Similarly, Andrea Evans-Massey, who was once married to her former *One Life to Live* costar Wayne Massey, dropped his name after they split.

When Bregman's onscreen mother, Susan Seaforth (JOANNA MANNING), married her leading man Bill Hayes (DOUG WILLIAMS, *Days of Our Lives*) she added his name to her own. She had been born Susan Seabold.

When Tonya Lee Williams (DR. OLIVIA BARBER) decided to become an actress, she learned that there was already a SAG member named Tanya Williams. She was advised to change her name in some way. Williams decided to add a middle name but ruled out using her own, Maxine, because she felt it was too long.

Sharon Farrell (FLO WEBSTER) was born with the last name Forthman.

A number of actors on the show have dropped their last names professionally, opting to use their middle names instead: Michael Damian [Weir], who played Danny Romalotti; Roberta Leighton [Weimar], who played Casey Reed; and Deborah Adair [Miller], one of the show's many Jill Abbotts.

Cynthia Eilbacher, who played April Stevens in the early 1980s, came back to Y&R in the early '90s with a new last name, Jordan. One of the factors that prompted the change was her career in stand-up comedy. She had grown weary of emcees mispronouncing her last name.

Devon Pierce, who played David Kimble's (Michael Corbett) partner-in-crime (and bed) Diane Westin, was born Ruth Zakarian.

When Ricky Paull Goldin (GARY DAWSON) was starting out as a child actor, his manager convinced him to drop his last name because it sounded too ethnic. Goldin used his middle name as his last name, adding an extra "L" to its original spelling. He did so partly to make it look more like a last name and partly to distance himself from his father, Paul Goldin, who had left Ricky and his mother years earlier. Eventually Goldin resumed using his last name but kept the unusual spelling of his middle name.

Like Eric Braeden, John McCook (LANCE PRENTISS) had been pressured by a studio executive into changing his name. Unlike Braeden, however, McCook was not given the opportunity to pick his new moniker. The name Bryan Cranston was assigned to him. When McCook discovered that there was already a Bryan Cranston in the actors' union, the studio executive relented and allowed him to use his real name.

When David Hasselhoff joined the cast, then-producer John Conboy suggested that a name change would be a good idea. "Anything you say," Hasselhoff replied. "I just want to keep the Hasselhoff."

AKA

1. What is Snapper Foster's real first name?
   (a) Edward   (c) David
   (b) William   (d) James

2. Which of the following characters went by the street name Kong while working as a mob enforcer?
   (a) Paul Williams   (c) Malcolm Winters
   (b) Nathan Hastings   (d) Andy Richards

3. Which of Katherine Chancellor's husbands was born Brian Romalotti?
   (a) Phillip Chancellor   (c) Rex Sterling
   (b) Derek Thurston   (d) none of them

---

4. When Tyrone Jackson infiltrated the mob, what name did he use?
   (a) Jack Tyler   (c) Tyler Johnson
   (b) Robert Tyrone   (d) T. J. Reynolds

5. Who published an unauthorized biography of Victor Newman under the pen name Nora Randall?
   (a) Jack Abbott   (c) Lorie Brooks
   (b) Traci Abbott   (d) Leanna Randolph

6. What is Cole Howard's (J. Eddie Peck) given first name?
   (a) Victor   (c) Charles
   (b) Nicholas   (d) Howard

7. By what name did a disguised David Kimble romance his mother-in-law, Flo Webster?
   (a) Jim Adams   (c) Red Carlton
   (b) Tim Brown   (d) Chris Donovan

8. When Paul Williams's father, Carl, was suffering from amnesia, what name did he use?
   (a) Charlie Wilson   (c) Will Carlson
   (b) Jim Bradley   (d) John Smith

9. When Veronica Landers took a job as Nikki's maid what name did she go by?
   (a) Sarah   (c) Marian
   (b) Alice   (d) Hazel

10. What character was born Christian Miller?
   (a) John Abbott   (c) Michael Baldwin
   (b) Brad Carlton   (d) Victor Newman

Happy Birthday to Them

January

4 Candice Daly (VERONICA LANDERS)

5 Ricky Paull Goldin (GARY DAWSON)

7 Camryn Grimes (CASSIE NEWMAN)

16 Josie Davis (GRACE TURNER)

18 David Lago (RAUL)

29 Marc Singer (CHET)

February

1 Vasili Bogazianos (AL FENTON)

3 Brenda Dickson (JILL FOSTER ABBOTT)

4 Stephanie Williams (AMY LEWIS)

8 Joshua Morrow (NICHOLAS NEWMAN)

9 Sharon Case (SHARON NEWMAN)

10 Sarah Aldrich (VICTORIA NEWMAN)

11 Stephen Gregory (CHASE BENSON)

18 Anthony Peña (MIGUEL RODRIGUEZ)

18 Jess Walton (JILL FOSTER ABBOTT)

March

1 Robert Clary (PIERRE ROULLAND)

9 Jaime Lyn Bauer (LORIE BROOKS)

16 Granville Van Dusen (KEITH DENNISON)

18 Marguerite Ray (MAMIE JOHNSON)

21 Logan Ramsey (JOSEPH ANTHONY)

23 Roberta Leighton (DR. CASEY REED)

23 David Tom (BILLY ABBOTT)

28 Todd Curtis (SKIP EVANS)

28 Janice Lynde (LESLIE BROOKS)

28 Siena Goines (CALLIE ROGERS)

29 Lauren Koslow (LINDSEY WELLS)

April

3 Eric Braeden (VICTOR NEWMAN)

3 Laura Bryan Birn (LYNNE BASSETT)

11 John Castellanos (JOHN SILVA)

13 Terry Lester (JACK ABBOTT)

18 Melody Thomas Scott (NIKKI REED NEWMAN)

20 Shemar Moore (MALCOLM WINTERS)

26 Michael Damian (DANNY ROMALOTTI)

May

2 Quinn Redeker (NICK REED and REX STERLING)

8 Julianne Morris (AMY WILSON)

10 Victoria Rowell (DRUCILLA BARBER WINTERS)

12 Beth Maitland (TRACI ABBOTT)

Mother's Day occasionally coincides with Victoria Rowell's (pictured here with daughter Maya) birthday.

© *Albert Ortega, Moonglow Photos*

14 Sabryn Genet (TRICIA DENNISON MCNEIL)

16 Scott Reeves (RYAN MCNEIL)

16 Nina Arvesen (CASSANDRA RAWLINS)

16 Carolyn Conwell (MARY WILLIAMS)

19 Steven Ford (ANDY RICHARDS)

19 Constance Towers (AUDREY NORTH)

22 Beau Kazer (BROCK REYNOLDS)

23 Deborah Adair (JILL FOSTER ABBOTT)

26 Tamara Clatterbuck (ALICE JOHNSON)

29 Tracey E. Bregman (LAUREN FENMORE)

29 Tom Selleck (JED ANDREWS)

31 Nick Scotti (TONY VISCARDI)

June

11 Peter Bergman (JACK ABBOTT)

13 Tom Hallick (DR. BRAD ELIOT)

15 Eileen Davidson (ASHLEY ABBOTT)

18 Andrea Evans (PATTY WILLIAMS ABBOTT)

18 Eddie Cibrian (MATT CLARK)

20 Brett Halsey (JOHN ABBOTT)

21 Leigh J. McCloskey (KURT COSTNER)

29 Kimberlin Brown (SHEILA CARTER)

July

4 Signy Coleman (HOPE ADAMS NEWMAN)

7 Cynthia [Eilbacher] Jordan (APRIL STEVENS)

11 Susan Seaforth Hayes (JOANNA MANNING)

15 Kristoff St. John (NEIL WINTERS)

17 David Hasselhoff (DR. SNAPPER FOSTER)

17 Tonya Lee Williams (DR. OLIVIA BARBER)

18 Darlene Conley (ROSE DEVILLE)

19 William Grey Espy (DR. SNAPPER FOSTER)

19 Peter Barton (DR. SCOTT GRAINGER)

19 Dennis Cole (LANCE PRENTISS)

20 Michael Corbett (DAVID KIMBLE)

26 Robert Colbert (STUART BROOKS)

31 Jay Bontatibus (TONY VISCARDI)

August

1 Jennifer Gareis (GRACE TURNER)

3 Heath Kizzier (DR. JOSHUA LANDERS)

6 Nathan Purdee (NATHAN "KONG" HASTINGS)

13 Alex Donnelley (DIANE JENKINS NEWMAN)

25 Christian LeBlanc (MICHAEL BALDWIN)

28 Marla Adams (DINA MERGERON)

September

3 Ashley Jones (MEGAN DENNISON)

5 Rod Arrants (DR. STEVEN LASSITER and JEFF)

7 John Phillip Law (DR. JIM GRAINGER)

9 Brenda Epperson Doumani (ASHLEY ABBOTT)

10 Tom Ligon (LUCAS PRENTISS)

12 Paul Walker (BRANDON COLLINS)

14 Michelle Stafford (PHYLLIS ROMALOTTI)

17 Aaron Lustig (DR. TIMOTHY REID)

23 Patty Weaver (GINA ROMA)

25 Josh Taylor (JED SANDERS)

29 Nicholas Pappone (PHILLIP CHANCELLOR MCNEIL)

October

4 Meg Bennett (JULIA NEWMAN)

5 Peter Brown (ROBERT LAURENCE)

10 J. Eddie Peck (COLE HOWARD)

10 Bond Gideon (JILL FOSTER)

12 Carlos Bernard (RAFAEL DELGADO)

Don Diamont was born on New Year's Eve.

© *Albert Ortega, Moonglow Photos*

16 Michael Tylo (BLADE and RICK BLADESON)

24 Doug Davidson (PAUL WILLIAMS)

24 Jon St. Elwood (JAZZ JACKSON)

25 Jeanne Cooper (KATHERINE CHANCELLOR)

28 Mark Derwin (ADRIAN HUNTER)

31 Deidre Hall (BARBARA ANDERSON)

November

2 Kate Linder (ESTHER VALENTINE)

4 Heather Tom (VICTORIA NEWMAN)

12 Jerry Douglas (JOHN ABBOTT)

14 Liz Keifer (ANGELA LAURENCE)

16 Tricia Cast (NINA WEBSTER MCNEIL)

18 Shari Shattuck (ASHLEY ABBOTT)

25 Amy Gibson (ALANA ANTHONY)

December

4 Donnelly Rhodes (PHILLIP CHANCELLOR II)

12 Wings Hauser (GREG FOSTER)

22 Lauralee Bell (CHRISTINE "CRICKET" BLAIR WILLIAMS)

24 Sharon Farrell (FLO WEBSTER)

27 Barbara Crampton (LEANNE LOVE)

29 Sandra Nelson (PHYLLIS ROMALOTTI)

30 Ashley Bashioum (MACKENZIE REYNOLDS)

31 Don Diamont (BRAD CARLTON)

Facts About the Stars

WHEN Y&R first began, the stars received more fan mail addressed to their characters than to themselves. Nowadays, fans not only know the actors' real names, they know after whom the actors were named and what they've named their pets and children.

HOME SWEET HOME

When creator/executive producer/head writer Bill Bell moved his family from Chicago to Los Angeles, he bought a home that had once been owned by billionaire Howard Hughes.

Among Eric Braeden's (Victor Newman) neighbors are Steven Spielberg and Sylvester Stallone.

Doug Davidson (Paul Williams), who is neighbors with Ted Danson and Mary Steenburgen, has attended barbecues at the home of another neighbor, comedian Dennis Miller.

Even after getting work on television, Christian LeBlanc (Michael Baldwin) kept his phone number listed—until mention was made in *Soap Opera Digest*.

Leigh McCloskey (KURT COSTNER) was once roommates with future *Frasier* star Kelsey Grammer.

At the extremely early age of thirteen, Amy Gibson (ALANA ANTHONY) moved out of her parents house and supported herself.

Because of financial difficulties, Heath Kizzier (DR. JOSHUA LANDERS) and his family lived for a year in a trio of tents.

John McCook's (LANCE PRENTISS) first apartment in New York City did not have its own bathroom. He had to use one down the hall with no electricity. One night, he lit a candle in the room only to notice a rat splashing around in the toilet.

NAMING NAMES

The J in J. Eddie Peck (COLE HOWARD) stands for John, his father's name.

Signy Coleman (HOPE NEWMAN) was named after a character in Swedish literature. Coleman named her daughter Siena after a city she visited in the Tuscany region of Italy while she was pregnant.

Shemar Moore (MALCOLM WINTERS) was named partly after his mother. The second syllable of his name is a shortened form of Marilyn.

Sabryn Genet's (TRICIA DENNISON MCNEIL) mother, a dancer, named her daughter after Sahyber Rawles, a dancer who has choreographed such films as *Staying Alive* and Warren Beatty's *Bugsy*. Genet's father modified the name from Sahyber to Sabryn.

Grant Cramer (SHAWN GARRETT and ADAM HUNTER) was named after his godfather, movie legend Cary Grant.

Although Tamara Clatterbuck (ALICE JOHNSON) was teased mercilessly about her name in school and encouraged by her varied agents to change it, she has kept it.

Alex Donnelley (DIANE JENKINS NEWMAN) suspected that Thorne Forrester on *The Bold and the Beautiful* was named after her first husband, Thorne Donnelley, whose family is friends with the Bells.

Aaron Lustig's (DR. TIM REID) mother nicknamed him Pussy.

Heath Kizzier (DR. JOSH LANDERS) was named after Heath Barkley, the character Lee Majors played on the 1960s Western series *The Big Valley.*

Kizzier's onscreen wife Candice Mia Daly (VERONICA LANDERS) was named after two Hollywood actresses: Candice Bergen and Mia Farrow.

Brody Hutzler's official first name is Ian, but he has always gone by his middle name, Brody. Only two people have ever called him Ian—his grandmother and a college professor whom he was too intimidated by to correct. His mother had wanted to name him Zachary, which, coincidentally, was the name of the character he played on *Guiding Light.*

Having grown up in Hong Kong, Elizabeth Sung (LUAN VOLIEN ABBOTT) went by two first names—one English, one Chinese. Her Chinese name, Fong, means "fragrant perfume."

ANIMAL MAGNETISM

Wolves are Scott Reeves's (RYAN MCNEIL) favorite animal. For Christmas one year, his brother sponsored a wolf pup being raised by a wildlife organization in Reeves's name.

Ricky Paull Goldin (GARY DAWSON) was once bitten by his pet boa constrictor.

Thom Bierdz (PHILLIP CHANCELLOR III) had a pet monkey named Debbie.

While growing up, Brenda Epperson (ASHLEY ABBOTT) kept a baby bull as a pet.

After a particularly difficult break-up, Sandra Nelson's (PHYLLIS ROMALOTTI) ex-boyfriend kidnapped her dog.

Jay Bontatibus (TONY VISCARDI) once jumped into New York City's notoriously polluted East River to save a puppy from drowning.

One morning, Candice Daly (VERONICA LANDERS) found her fish Joe floating at the top of his tank. Not one to give up that easy, she tried to jumpstart his heart by dowsing him in cold water. That didn't work, but she claims that he came back to life after he fell into her coffee.

MUSICAL TALENT

Doug Davidson (PAUL WILLIAMS) plays the bagpipes.

By age five, Terry Lester (JACK ABBOTT) had taught himself how to play the piano.

A classically trained trumpet player, Todd Curtis (SKIP EVANS) has apprenticed with both the Boston Symphony Orchestra and the Boston Pops.

Ellen Weston (SUZANNE LYNCH) wrote a song specifically for actress/singer Bernadette Peters to use in her cabaret act.

Tonya Lee Williams (DR. OLIVIA BARBER) can play four instruments: piano, violin, French horn, and tenor saxophone.

MEDICAL HISTORY

At the age of eighteen, Michelle Stafford (PHYLLIS ROMALOTTI) learned that she had a brain tumor. After talking to several doctors, she chose the one who promised that he could remove it without shaving her head. Instead, the surgeon pulled her face down to get at the tumor. Plastic surgery was then required to put her face back together.

While baking cookies at home, Sharon Farrell (FLO WEBSTER) burned her forehead so badly that the doctors recommended plastic surgery. Because she was heading under the knife anyway, she decided to have a complete facelift. That new face was banged up shortly thereafter when Farrell's car was involved in a head-on collision.

A bout of hepatitis, which she caught in a restaurant, put Meg Bennett's (JULIA NEWMAN) acting career on hold for approximately two years during the late 1970s. Doctors told her that the elimination of red meat from her diet years before had helped her fight the disease by taking strain off her liver.

John Considine (PHILLIP CHANCELLOR), who suffered from epilepsy as a teenager, played an epileptic on the Robert Young medical series *Marcus*

Welby, M.D. Considine wrote the script for the episode and created the epileptic character specifically for himself to play.

Colby Chester (MICHAEL CRAWFORD) suffers from dyslexia and has served as an administrator for a dyslexia treatment center in North Hollywood.

A bout of pneumonia forced Jeanne Cooper (KATHERINE CHANCELLOR) to quit smoking.

A car accident sent Todd Curtis (SKIP EVANS) crashing into the windshield. His badly scarred face required extensive plastic surgery. Curtis recovered from his numerous operations while continuing to act on the CBS soap opera *Capitol.*

Thom Bierdz (PHILLIP CHANCELLOR III) passed out from inhaling too many fumes while spray painting the refrigerator and stove in his apartment. He woke up long enough to phone for help. When the paramedics ultimately revived him, a disoriented Bierdz asked them if the "take" had gone well.

Phobic when it comes to germs, J. Eddie Peck (COLE HOWARD) refuses to touch anything in public bathrooms. He believes his precautions have paid off. He rarely catches colds or suffers from the flu.

RELIGIOUS FREEDOM

Frank Benard's (MARC MERGERON) mother wanted him to become a priest.

John O'Hurley (DR. JIM GRAINGER) considered entering the priesthood.

Although most Jewish men are bar mitzvahed in their early teens, Don Diamont (BRAD CARLTON) had his ceremony when he was in his thirties. After his father and brother died within a short period of time, Diamont grew interested in his heritage. Before his death, Diamont's father had expressed regret for not instilling in his children a better sense of their roots and religion.

Julianne Morris (AMY WILSON), whose parents were missionaries, taught Bible classes in a number of foreign countries.

Ashley Jones's (MEGAN DENNISON) father was a minister in the Church of Christ, a religion that prohibits drinking and dancing.

Patty Weaver's (GINA ROMA) father was a Pentecostal minister. She claims to have witnessed him heal people suffering from illnesses as serious as polio and emphysema.

HIGHER EDUCATION

Jerry Douglas (JOHN ABBOTT) has conducted a number of acting classes with prison inmates. By having the prisoners enact relationship-oriented scenes from Y&R scripts, Douglas has helped a number of them connect with long-buried emotions. Lauren Koslow (LINDSEY WELLS) occasionally accompanies Douglas on his visits.

Terry Lester (JACK ABBOTT), who could read the newspaper by age three, earned his undergraduate degree in political science.

Among Leigh McCloskey's (KURT COSTNER) classmates at Julliard was Robin Williams.

Anthony Herrera, who played college professor Jack Curtis, double-majored in English literature and zoology at the University of Mississippi.

Anthony Peña (MIGUEL RODRIGUEZ) also double-majored, studying both comparative literature and Native American history at California State University at Fullerton.

After getting a bachelor's degree in psychology, Robert Parucha (MATT MILLER) went on to earn a master's in East Asian philosophy.

Josh Taylor (JED SANDERS) holds a law degree from the University of Colorado.

Terrence McNally (ROBERT LYNCH) went to Harvard with Vice President Al Gore and film actor Tommy Lee Jones. At their twenty-fifth reunion, McNally directed Gore in a cabaret act.

Nick Scotti (TONY VISCARDI) left high school when he was sixteen.

FORMER OCCUPATIONS

Eric Braeden (VICTOR NEWMAN) worked on a ranch and in a lumber mill.

Nathan Purdee (NATHAN "KONG" HASTINGS) worked as a bounty hunter.

Candice Daly (VERONICA LANDERS) repossessed automobiles and trained dogs.

While still a teenager, J. Eddie Peck (COLE HOWARD) worked as a disc jockey at a radio station.

Like Peck, Deidre Hall (BARBARA ANDERSON) spun records for a radio station; unlike the station where Peck worked, Hall's was run solely by women.

Patty Weaver (GINA ROMA) shined shoes to pay for her acting classes.

Eric Braeden is a top-rated celebrity tennis player.

© Albert Ortega, Moonglow Photos

Peter Bergman (JACK ABBOTT) squeezed classes into a schedule that included two jobs. During the day, he raised money for cerebral palsy by phone; at night, he worked as a janitor.

John O'Hurley (DR. JIM GRAINGER) was a public relations director for the American Red Cross.

The daughter of a clothing designer, Amy Gibson (ALANA ANTHONY) made money between her gigs on Y&R and General Hospital by designing a line of beaded brassieres.

Prior to landing acting roles, Quinn Redeker worked in a wide variety of jobs, including dance teacher, fisherman, interior decorator, truck driver, and police officer.

In her native Norway, Nina Arvesen (CASSANDRA RAWLINS) subtitled American films, ran a television station, and opened up the country's first RCA/Motown affiliate.

For many years, Kate Linder (ESTHER VALENTINE) juggled her acting career with a job as a flight attendant. For the first two years of her employment on The Young and the Restless, she kept her career as a flight attendant secret, fearing that the soap's producers might question her commitment to her acting career. Linder's secret came out after her onscreen boss, Jeanne Cooper (KATHERINE CHANCELLOR), bought a seat on one of her flights. By the next day, everyone at CBS knew of Kate's second job.

SPORTS AND EXERCISE

Tennis magazine once ranked Eric Braeden (VICTOR NEWMAN) as the top celebrity player. He has played an exhibition match against tennis great Monica Seles. His soccer team, the Maccabees, won the 1972 National Soccer Championship.

Phil Morris (TYRONE JACKSON) was coached in track by Dwight Stones, who had won a bronze medal for the high jump at the 1972 Summer Olympics and a silver medal in 1976.

Doug Davidson (PAUL WILLIAMS) holds a black belt in karate.

Jennifer Gareis (GRACE TURNER) began swimming when she was three and competing when she was five. In college, she was named NCAA All-American in the butterfly competition and ranked among the top five in the nation in her category.

Andre Khabbazi (ALEC MORETTI) has played tennis semi-professionally.

Peter Brown (ROBERT LAURENCE) has competed in rodeos, organized charity rodeos, and filmed an instructional video on penning cattle from a rushing herd.

Kristoff St. John (NEIL WINTERS) manages his ex-wife Mia "The Knockout" St. John's boxing and kickboxing career. He has also made an instructional kickboxing video entitled *Kick Butt*.

While attending college on a baseball scholarship, Shemar Moore (MALCOLM WINTERS) was scouted by such teams as the Milwaukee Brewers and the Boston Red Sox.

THE ARMED FORCES

Terry Lester (JACK ABBOTT) learned and taught Russian in the U.S. Army.

Peter Brown (ROBERT LAURENCE) organized an army theater group while stationed in Alaska.

An eighteen-month army stint delayed Frank Benard's (MARC MERGERON) plans to move from France to Hollywood.

Quinn Redeker (NICK REED and REX STERLING) enlisted in the Marine Corps and later joined the Air Force Cadets.

During the Vietnam War, John McCook (LANCE PRENTISS) played piano and conducted the men's chorus while serving in the army. Playing piano literally saved his life. Prior to winning that position, McCook was being trained as a radio man—a position with a life expectancy in combat of roughly two weeks.

Here She Comes . . .

Kimberlin Brown (SHEILA CARTER) represented California in the Miss USA pageant.

Tonya Lee Williams (DR. OLIVIA BARBER) was once named Miss Black Ontario.

Devon Pierce (DIANE WESTIN) was named Miss Teen USA.

Brenda Epperson (ASHLEY ABBOTT) was named Miss Oregon United Teenager and Miss Fire Prevention.

Jaime Lyn Bauer (LORIE BROOKS) was once named Junior Miss Phoenix and made it to the finals of the Miss Arizona pageant. After moving to Chicago, she was named Miss Chicago and was second runner-up for the title of Miss Illinois.

Michelle Thomas (CALLIE ROGERS) was crowned queen in an international pageant held in Jamaica in 1985. While competing, she met future Y&R cast mate Kristoff St. John (NEIL WINTERS).

Deidre Hall (BARBARA ANDERSON) was named Junior Orange Bowl Queen.

Joy Garrett (BOOBSIE CASWELL) was once named Miss Fort Worth.

Sharon Farrell (FLO WEBSTER) was named both Miss Brooklyn and Miss Manhattan.

Being a runner-up in the Miss Hollywood Pageant earned Sabryn Genet (TRICIA DENNISON) free acting lessons.

Naked Ambition

Jaime Lyn Bauer (LAURALEE BROOKS) was not only part of a 1982 *Playboy* pictorial on soap actresses, she was the only one who allowed full frontal nudity. Ironically, she told the magazine that she would prefer not to be doing so many sex scenes on Y&R.

Roberta Leighton (DR. CASEY REED) appeared in the same pictorial as Bauer but wore a see-through teddy.

Barbara Crampton (LEANNE LOVE) posed topless in a feature pictorial that spoofed her career as a horror film actress.

John Gibson, who played stripper Jerry "Cash" Cashman, was one of the only soap actors to bare it all for *Playgirl*.

During his days as a male model, Nick Scotti (TONY VISCARDI) appeared nude in a number of fashion layouts.

Michelle Thomas (CALLIE ROGERS) turned down several offers from various magazines to pose nude.

BRUSHES WITH CELEBRITY

While taking a tour of the White House, Eric Braeden (VICTOR NEWMAN) met then President Ronald Reagan on the helicopter pad as Reagan was heading off to Camp David. As Braeden was meeting the president, a busload of schoolchildren started yelling "Victor! Victor!" out of their windows.

Diana Barton (MARI JO MASON) was so flustered upon meeting President Clinton and his wife Hillary at a fundraising event that she literally forgot her own name.

Colleen Casey (FARREN CONNOR) once serenaded President Ronald Reagan and his wife, Nancy, at a Congressional Ball.

Frank Benard (MARC MERGERON) worked as the personal photographer for the internationally renowned surrealist painter Salvador Dali.

Walt Disney himself complimented John McCook (LANCE PRENTISS) after listening to him narrate the Jungle Cruise ride at Disneyland.

Grant Cramer (SHAWN GARRETT and ADAM HUNTER) was never much impressed meeting the guests at parties given by his mother, movie star Terry Moore—even though they included such show business legends as John Wayne and Cary Grant.

Back when Jess Walton (JILL ABBOTT) was hanging around with rock-and-roll types, Helen Reddy ("I Am Woman") taught her how to play chess.

Although Lynne Topping (CHRIS BROOKS) did not know *Three's Company* star John Ritter personally, he was the first person she told about her pregnancy. The two shared an elevator shortly after Topping learned that she was expecting a baby. She was acting so oddly on the elevator that Ritter asked her repeatedly if she was feeling all right. She finally confessed to him the reason for her excitement.

Rock music fan Tricia Cast (NINA MCNEIL) could not speak when she met Robert Plant from the legendary group Led Zeppelin. She just threw herself against a wall and fell down laughing.

Back when *Charlie's Angels* was still on the air, Michael Damian (DANNY ROMALOTTI) saw one of the show's stars, Jaclyn Smith, in a bookstore. Nervous, he spent a good twenty minutes trying to work up the courage to ask her for her autograph—by which time she had already left.

CRIME AND PUNISHMENT

Peter Bergman (JACK ABBOTT) shared an apartment in one of New York City's more dangerous neighborhoods. After the third time the place was burglarized within a single year, Bergman and his roommates decided to move.

Bergman's onscreen wife Elizabeth Sung (LUAN VOLIEN ABBOTT) had her own brush with crime while living in New York. One night, while she was waiting for a taxi, three men jumped out of a car. One of them was carrying a gun, and they demanded her money. She gave them what they wanted and was not harmed.

Shemar Moore (MALCOLM WINTERS), who once had his luggage stolen by a taxi driver, had his jacket stolen in the subway by a thief who pretended to shove a gun in his back. The gun turned out to be nothing more than the hood's fist.

Patty Weaver (GINA ROMA), who was physically abused by her first husband, helped form the Coalition of Battered Women.

The break-up of one of her relationships got so out of hand that Candice Daly (VERONICA LANDERS) not only filed a restraining order against an ex-boyfriend, she also bought a gun.

PEOPLE WHO READ PEOPLE

The first *People* magazine cover story devoted to the daytime soaps featured Jaime Lyn Bauer (LORIE BROOKS) as well as two future *Y&R* actors: Peter Bergman (JACK ABBOTT), then playing Dr. Cliff Warner on *All My Children,* and Josh Taylor (JED SANDERS), then playing Chris Kostichek on *Days of Our Lives.*

Don Diamont (BRAD CARLTON) was the first daytime soap opera actor to make *People* magazine's list of the 50 Most Beautiful People in the World.

Diamont's onscreen wife Nina Arvesen (CASSANDRA RAWLINS) was also considered for that honor.

In 1997, Eileen Davidson (ASHLEY ABBOTT) was less than thrilled to land a spot on *People* magazine's list of the ten worst-dressed women.

I'D LIKE TO BUY A VOWEL

At the age of eleven, Kristoff St. John (NEIL WINTERS) auditioned for *The Gong Show.* He sang the John Denver classic "Sunshine on My Shoulders" and accompanied himself on the guitar. The producers considered his act neither good enough nor bad enough to put him on air.

Doug Davidson (PAUL WILLIAMS) hosted a short-lived nighttime version of *The Price Is Right.*

Tonya Lee Williams (DR. OLIVIA BARBER) once auditioned to become a model on *The Price Is Right.*

Melody Thomas Scott (NIKKI NEWMAN) is one of the few daytime actors who has competed during the celebrity tournaments on *Jeopardy.*

Although Andrea Evans (PATTY WILLIAMS) never appeared on *Jeopardy,* she was thrilled when her name was used as an answer.

In the mid-1980s, Scott Reeves competed on a game show called *Press Your Luck.* He came close to winning $9,000 in cash and a trip to Singapore, but he pressed his luck too far and went home with a consolation prize instead.

Before joining the cast of *Y&R,* Laura Bryan Birn (LYNNE BASSETT) competed on *Wheel of Fortune.*

Lauralee Bell (CHRISTINE WILLIAMS) did so well during a celebrity edition of *Wheel of Fortune* that she made it into the bonus round, which she knew would make her late for dinner with her publicist. Her preoccupation with the dinner worked in her favor; the solution to the final puzzle was PUBLICIST.

Unscripted Kisses

WHILE PLAYING doctors in love Snapper Foster and Casey Reed, David Hasselhoff and Roberta Leighton went through an on again/off again relationship of their own. The two were engaged at three different times but never made it down the aisle.

During the 1980s, Hasselhoff did get married to another soap opera actress, Catherine Hickland, who has worked on *Capitol*, *Loving/The City*, and *One Life to Live*. That union ended in 1987. Hasselhoff is presently married to actress Pamela Bach, who originated the role of Mari Jo Mason, Jack Abbott's love interest and Victor Newman's would-be killer.

Roberta Leighton is currently married to another soap doctor, Corey Young, who played Dr. Walt Benson on *General Hospital*. The two were fixed up by their mutual publicist when Leighton needed an escort for a charity benefit. Between Hasselhoff and Young, Leighton dated *Y&R* alum Tony Geary (GEORGE CURTIS) whom she met while working on *General Hospital* in the early 1980s.

Jaime Lyn Bauer (LORIE BROOKS PRENTISS) has been married for many years to Jeremy Swan, a former make-up artist for *Y&R*. Bauer did not even realize that Swan was interested in her until after she performed a bellydancing scene. She learned from a third party that Swan was quite taken not only with her performance but with her costume as well. Bauer then flirted with Swan whenever she sat down in his make-up chair. The two kept their relationship a secret in the beginning because CBS frowned upon its employees dating one another.

Lauren Koslow (LINDSEY WELLS) was under the impression that Nick Schillace, head of make-up for CBS daytime, didn't care much for her. Therefore, she managed to avoid sitting in his chair up until the point when the producers decided that Lindsey needed a new look. The responsibility of creating that look was assigned to Schillace. From that point on, Schillace did Koslow's make-up every day. Over time the two became good friends. It took them a little while longer to admit that they were falling in love. Schillace took a long time to admit his attraction. Along the way, he merely offered his opinion on whom she should and shouldn't be dating. The couple eventually married.

Although Melody Thomas Scott (NIKKI NEWMAN) did not marry make-up artist Carlos Yeaggy, the two did live together and had a child together, in

Melody Thomas Scott and her real-life leading man, executive producer Ed Scott.
© *Sue Schneider,*
Moonglow Photos

1983. Three years later, Scott wed Y&R's current executive producer Ed Scott. The two have been married for thirteen years and counting. Some actors have found it a little intimidating playing opposite the producer's wife—especially in love scenes. Scott once needed to give J. Eddie Peck (Cole Howard) permission and encouragement to "turn up the heat" during a love scene between Cole and Nikki.

Doug Davidson (Paul Williams) met his wife, Cindy Fisher, back in the early 1980s when she had a short-term role on the show as a cult member. Years later, Fisher returned to the show in a short-term gig as Paul's blind date, Dana Nielsen. Before meeting Fisher, Davidson dated Genie Francis while she was at the height of her popularity as Laura on *General Hospital*.

Scott Reeves (Ryan McNeil) met his wife Melissa [Brennan] Reeves while working on *Days of Our Lives*. At the time, Brennan was the show's centerpiece heroine. She shared only one scene with Reeves, but he couldn't help but take notice. After his run with the show ended, he continued to visit the set. During one of those visits, Reeves copped Brennan's phone number from a cast list and invited her to a small party at his apartment that evening. The two immediately fell into a relationship. Within two months, Reeves took her on a limousine ride and presented her with an engagement ring.

Ricky Paull Goldin (Gary Dawson) considers Melissa Reeves his first real love. After losing her, he dated her *Days of Our Lives* cast mate Charlotte Ross for a few months. Among his more notable celebrity girlfriends has been Yasmine Bleeth (*Baywatch, Nash Bridges*), whom he met while working on a play in which her character dumps his.

Julianne Morris (Amy Wilson) and Eddie Cibrian (Matt Clark) began dating while their characters were romantically involved on the show. Morris, who had broken up with talk show/game show host Mike Berger because of religious differences, had gone public with her decision to remain a virgin until she married. Although she understood that Cibrian was not a virgin, he had promised to refrain from sex until their wedding night. After roughly two and a half years of dating, Cibrian met with Morris's parents secretly to discuss his plans to propose. Although Morris's parents gave their blessing, Cibrian and Morris broke up two weeks later. Morris has described the relationship as nothing more than a facade and has intimated during interviews with the soap press that Cibrian did not keep his promise of celibacy.

For the past four years, Patty Weaver (GINA ROMA) has been married to Jerry Birn, a writer from the show.

For several years, John McCook (LANCE PRENTISS) was married to famed singer–actress Juliet Prowse, ten years his senior. Today, McCook is married to actress Laurette Spang, best known to sci-fi fans as Cassiopeia in the 1970s space series *Battlestar Gallactica*.

Dennis Cole took over the role of Lance Prentiss while he was in the midst of divorcing Jaclyn Smith, who was starring at the time on the primetime detective series *Charlie's Angels*.

While Quinn Redeker (NICK REED and REX STERLING) was playing the villainous Alex Marshall on *Days of Our Lives,* he fell in love with the show's leading lady, *Y&R* alumna Deidre Hall (BARBARA ANDERSON). The two dated for several years, during which time Hall is reported to have gotten jealous over Redeker's love scenes with other actresses.

Peter Bergman (JACK ABBOTT) has admitted that he was too young when he married comic actress Christine Ebersole, who has worked on daytime (*Ryan's Hope, One Life to Live*), *Saturday Night Live,* and in feature films including the Macaulay Culkin comedy *Richie Rich*. He met his current wife, Mariellen, through his *All My Children* cast mate Michael Minor.

Nathan Purdee (NATHAN HASTINGS) and Stephanie Williams (AMY LEWIS) first met at the American Black Achievement Awards, but it wasn't until years later, when they were paired opposite each other on *Y&R* as lovers, that a real-life romance blossomed. Years after their romance had run its course, they were paired onscreen again as husband and wife in the ABC soap opera *One Life to Live.*

Tricia Cast (Nina Webster McNeil) is married to Jack Allocco, who composes music for both *Y&R* and *B&B.* Alloco titled one such composition "For Tricia."

Prior to marrying Cast, Alloco was once engaged to Tracey E. Bregman. It was one of several romances Bregman found on the set. Shortly after she joined the show, Bregman fell for Randy Holland, who played Nikki's homicidal boyfriend Rick Daros. Several years before Bregman had joined the cast, mutual friends had tried to pair her with Holland. Bregman did not meet Holland, though, until after she landed the role of Lauren Fenmore. Her first glimpse of him was on a monitor screen, and she was taken by his good looks. When they finally worked together, they hit it off immediately. Bregman knew that the relationship was something special when Holland picked her up in a red truck. Prior to meeting him, a psychic had predicted that she would date a man who drove a red truck.

Although Bregman never dated Josh Taylor (Jed Sanders) while the two worked together on *Days of Our Lives,* they had a crush on one another. Taylor did not blame their failure to connect as a couple so much on the ten-year age gap between them—he was in his mid-twenties, Bregman was a teenager—so much as their strong ambition to build show business careers. Taylor once told *Soap Opera Digest:* "We could have had something."

Bregman also had a cross-country romance with Tom Eplin, who played Jake McKinnon on the New York–produced *Another World.* Just when it looked as though Bregman and Eplin were headed toward marriage, Eplin dumped her for his then roommate and costar Ellen Wheeler.

Vincent Irizarry (Dr. David Hayward, *All My Children*) has been involved with two of Victor Newman's ex-wives. He married Signy Coleman

(HOPE NEWMAN), who was his leading lady on *Santa Barbara*. An onscreen romance between Irizarry and Barbara Crampton (LEANNE LOVE) on *Guiding Light* briefly evolved into the real thing.

K. T. Stevens (VANESSA PRENTISS) was married for more than twenty years to Hugh Marlowe, best known to *Another World* fans as Jim Matthews, a role he began shortly after their divorce.

Michael Tylo (BLADE and RICK BLADESON) has been married for several years to Hunter Tylo (DR. TAYLOR HAYES, *The Bold and the Beautiful*). The two met while working together on the ABC soap opera *All My Children*. The first time they met, Hunter (then going by the name Deborah Morehart) could not stand Tylo. Because all of Hunter's serious relationships began with an instant dislike for her future mates, she believed she and Tylo were probably bound for some kind of relationship. Michael Tylo believes that their real-life romance led to Hunter's dismissal from *All My Children*.

On *The Bold and the Beautiful*, Hunter Tylo is married to Ronn Moss aka Ridge Forrester. Moss's wife, Shari Shattuck, took over the role of Blade's widow Ashley Abbott after Tylo had left the show. Shattuck and Moss met while working together on an HBO film titled *Hot Child in the City*. Just as Hunter Tylo's immense popularity on *B&B* did not assure her husband job security on *Y&R,* neither did Moss's popularity keep his wife from getting fired.

Replacing Shattuck as Ashley was Eileen Davidson, who originated the role and who had a slew of high-profile romances. Back in the 1980s, she dated Nicholas Walker when he was working on *Capitol*. Walker did a short turn on *Y&R* as Jason Monroe. After breaking up with Walker, Davidson was briefly married to Chip Mayer, who played Vance Duke on *The Dukes of Hazzard* and TJ on *Santa Barbara*. She also dated movie star Jon Voight, with whom she worked on the film *Eternity*. She is presently married to Jon Lindstrom, who stars on *Port Charles*. Lindstrom, it should be noted, has played twin brothers on *General Hospital* while Davidson portrayed quadruplets on *Days of Our Lives.*

One of Davidson's more prominent romances was with Don Diamont, who plays Brad Carlton on the show. When she first met him, she found him much too cocky for her liking. It wasn't until she left the show and came back to visit friends on the set that she got to know him better, and the two started dating. It was also after Davidson left the show that Brad got involved with Ashley.

**In between stints as Ashley Abbott, Eileen Davidson
dated costar Don Diamont.**
© *Albert Ortega, Moonglow Photos*

Prior to Davidson, Diamont had been involved in a high-profile affair with soap actress–singer Gloria Loring, whom he met while playing her lover on *Days of Our Lives*. Like Davidson, Loring was turned off by Diamont's cocky attitude the first time they met. Playing onscreen lovers, however, gave way to the real thing despite a sixteen-year age difference. Diamont and Loring initially kept their relationship a secret because Loring was still married to *Growing Pains* star Alan Thicke.

John O'Hurley (DR. JIM GRAINGER) was once married to Eva La Rue, who shot to daytime fame playing Dr. Maria Santos on *All My Children*.

O'Hurley's onscreen son Peter Barton (DR. SCOTT GRAINGER) went out with Lisa Rinna for three years before she made it big on *Days of Our Lives* and later *Melrose Place*. His other Hollywood romances included Nicolette Sheridan, who played Paige Matheson on *Knots Landing*. Ironically both women have been married to *L.A. Law* star Harry Hamlin. Barton himself almost married Kimberly Beck, who played Julie Clegg on *Capitol*. Future *Sisters* star Julianne Phillips dumped him for rock giant Bruce Springsteen. Years before their characters were paired up on *Y&R*, Tracey E. Bregman had developed a crush on Barton, whom she knew only from his varied TV appearances.

Michelle Stafford (PHYLLIS ROMALOTTI) briefly dated Michael Dietz, who played Dr. Joe Scanlon on *Port Charles*.

Diana Barton (MARI JO MASON) has been romantically linked to such Hollywood heavyweights as Jack Nicholson and Warren Beatty.

Lauralee Bell (CHRISTINE "CRICKET" BLAIR) dated a couple of her leading men, namely Michael Damian (DANNY ROMALOTTI) and Stephen Gregory (CHASE BENSON). Although Christine's plotlines crossed with Nicholas Newman's (Josh Morrow) only as lawyer/client, Bell and Morrow also went out. Among Bell's other celebrity dates have been: Scott Baio (*Happy Days, Charles in Charge*); Brian Bloom (DUSTY DONOVAN, *As the World Turns*); Curt McCown from the teen comedy *Can't Buy Me Love*;

and John Preston (GREG HOWARD, *General Hospital*), whom she met through their mutual publicist.

Andrea Evans (PATTY WILLIAMS ABBOTT) was married to country singer/actor Wayne Massey, whom she met while working together on *One Life to Live*. They left the show together and headed out to Los Angeles, where they eventually split.

Rod Arrants (DR. STEVEN LASSITER) was once married to Patricia Estrin, whom he met while they were playing brother and sister on the short lived soap opera *Lovers and Friends*.

Jess Walton (JILL FOSTER ABBOTT) was once married to Bruce Davison, who has been Oscar-nominated for his work in the AIDS drama *Longtime Companion*. Most recently he was hired to play a mutant-hating senator in the big screen adaptation of the X-Men comic books.

Shemar Moore (MALCOLM WINTERS) became involved with film actress Halle Berry shortly after her divorce from baseball star Dave Justice. Too soon, it turned out. Berry was not ready to get into another relationship, but the two have remained friends.

For six years, the late Michelle Thomas (CALLIE ROGERS) dated Malcolm Jamal Warner, who played Bill Cosby's son Theo on *The Cosby Show*. Thomas occasionally guest-starred on *The Cosby Show* as Theo's girlfriend Justine. Although she considered him the love of her life, she blamed their break-up on their youth and their need to grow as individuals.

Victoria Rowell (DRUCILLA WINTERS) has a child with jazz musician Wynton Marsalis.

Dax Griffin, who played Tim Truman on the recently canceled *Sunset Beach*, used to go out with Josie Davis, who originated the role of Grace Turner. Davis was replaced by Jennifer Gareis not only in the role of Grace but in Griffin's heart as well. In an ironic romantic twist, Griffin has recently been dating Gareis.

Real-Life Wedding Album

MELODY THOMAS Scott (NIKKI NEWMAN) was married to her first husband by the man who would become her second husband. The two actually knew each other from medical school. Neither of the two unions lasted longer than six months.

Brain surgery forced Scott Reeves (RYAN MCNEIL) and his wife Melissa (JENNIFER HORTON, *Days of Our Lives*) to postpone their wedding. A sinus infection had deteriorated into an abscess, which at one point the doctors worried might be a tumor. After Reeves survived the surgery, he and Melissa began replanning their wedding, though on a far less grand scale. Rather than plan another 300-guest affair that would take six months to pull together, they decided to get married as soon as possible and did so in front of forty family members and close friends. Because Melissa Reeves had already used up vacation time on the wedding and honeymoon that didn't happen, she had to work on the day she finally married Scott. She even drove herself to the ceremony, wearing her wedding dress.

Tired of dating actors, Lauralee Bell called up Scott Martin, a classmate from elementary school, to take her to the 1996 *Soap Opera Digest* Awards. Although Martin still lived in Chicago, where he and Bell grew up, he flew out to Los Angeles for the ceremony. Bell was impressed with his adventurous soul; during the visit, the two got tattooed. She also liked the ease with which he handled all the press attention. When the time came time for him to return to Chicago, she went along. Within two years, Bell and Martin were married. While dating, Martin discovered his high school yearbook, in which Bell had once written: " . . . if you have a good summer job, I'll expect my engagement ring soon."

Shortly after Tricia Cast announced her engagement to the show's music director Jack Allocco, the two secretly eloped to Las Vegas. The honeymoon was short-lived. The two headed back to Los Angeles the very next morning so that Cast could tape her scenes for the day. Cast members, who didn't realize that they had tied the knot, spent the day coming up to Cast to congratulate her on her engagement.

Although Michael Damian (DANNY ROMALOTTI) and Janeen Best eloped to Las Vegas, he wanted to give his bride an old-fashioned wedding—very old in fact. The two headed to France to exchange vows in a twelfth century church. Their reception was then held in a fifteenth century chateau. The bride's wedding ring, which had been created in the 1920s, had once belonged to Best's mother. On the day of the ceremony, to make sure that he didn't see his bride before the church, Damian organized a golf game for himself and fifteen friends.

When Jerry Douglas (JOHN ABBOTT) married KABC news reporter Kymberly Banks, the wedding was a star-studded affair. In attendance were three of Douglas's onscreen wives: Marla Adams (DINA MERGERON) as well as two Jills, Brenda Dickson and Deborah Adair. Patty Weaver (GINA ROMA) sang for the guests. The wedding took place at the Mountaingate Country Club, which had been used as Fallon's hotel La Mirage on *Dynasty*. Even the chauffeur was a celebrity. Former child star Paul Petersen, who worked on *The Donna Reed Show*, ran the limousine company and opted to drive for Douglas and his new bride.

So heavy were the rains the day John McCook (LANCE PRENTISS) married Laurette Spang that both the bride and groom arrived late.

While vacationing in Tahiti, Lauren Koslow (LINDSEY WELLS) and make-up artist Nick Schillace decided to finally tie the knot. In keeping with local customs, they consulted with a tribal elder about the day and time when they should hold the ceremony. Although it was raining the day they planned to be wed, the elder promised that the weather would clear up at four o'clock. Trusting his wisdom, Koslow and Schillace headed out on a catamaran to be married at sea. Just as the elder promised, the skies cleared up right at four o'clock.

Sharon Farrell (FLO WEBSTER) has been married a total of four times. The first of those marriages took place while she was only sixteen years old and lasted only two weeks.

When John Considine, who originated the role of Katherine Chancellor's late husband Phillip, married his wife Astrid, the 1984 wedding came as no small surprise to their family and friends. While hosting a Christmas Eve party in his home, Considine announced that he was getting married to Astrid, made a joke about hating long engagements, then sprung the real surprise on everyone: They were getting married right then and there.

In a pseudo-incestuous twist that would fit perfectly into the Y&R landscape, Alex Donnelley's (DIANE JENKINS) first husband was also her stepuncle. Her mother was married to his half-brother.

Brenda Dickson (JILL FOSTER ABBOTT) incorporated real live swans into her Christmas Day wedding to lawyer Jan Weinberg. Dickson selected the swans not only for their beauty but also for their reputation in the animal kingdom of mating for life.

While David Hasselhoff (DR. SNAPPER FOSTER) was dating Capitol's Catherine Hickland, she wrote an episode for Knight Rider in which his character Michael Knight was reunited with his ex-fiancée Stevie. The last day taping that episode coincided with Hickland's birthday. Hasselhoff commemorated the dual event with a marriage proposal. After Hickland and Hasselhoff married in real life, she filmed a Knight Rider in which Michael married Stevie. At one point, Hickland considered wearing the same dress in which she had wed Hasselhoff but changed her mind when she realized that it could be ruined during some of the varied stunts planned for the show. Instead, three copies of her wedding dress were made: one for her, one for the stuntwoman, and an extra in case it was needed. The same pastor who had married Hasselhoff and Hickland guested on the show to join Stevie and Michael in holy matrimony.

Don Diamont (BRAD CARLTON) interrupted his honeymoon to audition for a deodorant commercial. Diamont's agent called to let him know that Sure was interested in hiring him for a TV spot; he then faxed Diamont the script he would have to learn. Diamont and his new bride rented a video camera and taped Diamont saying his lines in their hotel bathroom.

Isn't It Romantic?

1. Why did Snapper Foster sleep with Sally McGuire while he was engaged to Chris Brooks?
(a) Chris refused to have sex until the wedding night.
(b) Jill lied to Snapper that Chris was sleeping around.
(c) Sally was paying him for sex.
(d) In a drunken stupor, Snapper mistook Sally for Chris.

2. Where did Jill Abbott marry Phillip Chancellor?
(a) in the Chancellor mansion
(b) on a cruise ship
(c) in his hospital room
(d) in Las Vegas

3. Who plotted to kill Lorie Brooks after she married millionaire Lance Prentiss?
(a) her sister Leslie
(b) Jill Foster
(c) Lance's mother, Vanessa
(d) Lance himself

4. What movie theme is Victor Newman and Nikki Reed's signature love song?

(a) "Evergreen" from *A Star Is Born*

(b) "Through the Eyes of Love" from *Ice Castles*

(c) "How Deep Is Your Love" from *Saturday Night Fever*

(d) "If You Could Read My Mind" from *Superman*

5. For what crime did Paul Williams first arrest Lauren Fenmore?

(a) speeding

(b) stealing a car

(c) shoplifting

(d) drug possession

6. In what capacity was Brad Carlton working for the Abbott family when he first met Traci?

(a) house painter

(b) stable boy

(c) chauffeur

(d) gardener

7. Which of the following was not a secret that Rex Sterling hid from Katherine Chancellor when he first began courting her?

(a) He was Danny Romalotti's father.

(b) He was an alcoholic.

(c) Jill Abbott paid him to woo Katherine.

(d) He had served time in prison.

8. Who gave Christine away when she married Danny Romalotti?

(a) her father, Jim Grainger

(b) her brother, Scott Grainger

(c) her mother, Jessica Blair

(d) her stepfather, John Abbott

9. Why did Drucilla Barber, who eventually married Neil Winters, originally try to pair him up with her sister Olivia?

(a) Drucilla wanted Olivia's boyfriend, Nathan.

(b) Drucilla wanted to break Olivia's heart by stealing Neil back.

(c) Olivia needed to be married to collect their grandfather's inheritance.

(d) Neil offered her $10,000 to find him the perfect wife.

10. With what Biblical name did Nicholas and Sharon Newman christen their son?

(a) Aaron

(b) Isaac

(c) Noah

(d) Moses

Family Business

THE ONLY two daytime dramas that can truly be considered family businesses are *The Young and the Restless* and *The Bold and the Beautiful*. Bill Bell created *The Young and the Restless* back in the early 1970s with his wife, Lee Phillip Bell. Over the years, each of their three children have become closely involved with the shows. Bell's daughter Lauralee has been playing its centerpiece young heroine, Christine aka Cricket, since 1983. Bradley Bell has worked behind the scenes with his father, writing the two shows. Ever since he was in high school, Bradley would sit in on writers' meetings with his father and crew. He recently ascended to become *B&B*'s head writer. William Bell Jr. meanwhile works in the business end of the two series.

Lauralee Bell's good friend Laura Bryan Birn (LYNNE BASSETT) joined the show shortly after her father, Jerry Birn, signed on as a writer. Jerry Birn's marriage to Patty Weaver (GINA ROMA) makes Weaver Laura Bryan Birn's stepmother.

Jeanne Cooper (KATHERINE CHANCELLOR) has played mother to her own son, actor Corbin Bernsen, a number of times, most notably on his hit legal drama *L.A. Law*. Cooper also played Bernsen's mother in the feature film comedy *Frozen Assets*. Also in that film was Cooper's other son, Collin, who has landed small roles in a number of films, among them the Jim Belushi–Linda Hamilton romantic fantasy *Mr. Destiny*. Cooper's daughter Carin has also been seen on the big screen. In 1967, at the age of seven, she made her film debut in *The Trip*, a Peter Fonda–Dennis Hopper film about a TV director's first experiment with LSD.

Bill Bell and Lee Phillip Bell with their daughter, Lauralee.
© *Albert Ortega, Moonglow Photos*

Steven Ford, who played Andy Richards, is the son of former U.S. president Gerald Ford. In 1987, former president Ford visited the *Y&R* studio.

As a child, Philip Morris (Tyrone Jackson) loved to visit the set of the 1960s spy series *Mission: Impossible,* where his father Greg Morris starred as electronics whiz Barney Collier. In the late '80s, when the series was revived, Phil Morris played Barney's son, Grant, also an electronics whiz. Morris has also guested once as a basketball player on an episode of *Vega$,* the 1970s detective series on which his father played police lieutenant David Nelson.

Kristoff St. John's (Neil Winters) father is actor Christopher St. John, best remembered for his work in the 1971 crime drama *Shaft.* The elder St. John has appeared on *Y&R* a number of times over the years as a minister. He married Nathan and Olivia (Nathan Purdee and Tonya Lee Williams), baptized their son, and married Neil and Drucilla (Victoria Rowell). Before *Y&R,* the St. Johns had worked together, playing father and son on the short-lived '70s series *The Bad News Bears.*

John Considine's (Phillip Chancellor) father, John W. Considine Jr., produced more than forty films, among them the Rudolph Valentino silent film classic *The Son of the Sheik* and the Spencer Tracy drama *Boys Town.* While Considine was growing up, he would occasionally accompany his father to the studio and run movies for him. On television, Considine's younger brother Tim starred as Spin in the Mickey Mouse Club Western *Spin and Marty;* Tim Considine also played Mike Douglas, one of *My Three Sons* in the Fred MacMurray sitcom.

Tracey Bregman's (Lauren Fenmore) father Buddy Bregman produced a number of films during the 1950s and '60s, including the Jerry Lewis comedy *The Delicate Delinquent.* He and Tracey Bregman's mother, actress Suzanne Lloyd, have worked as extras on *Y&R.* Viewers have seen Buddy Bregman playing the piano and Lloyd dancing in the background of various scenes. Tracey Bregman's uncle Jules Styne composed the music for such Broadway musicals as *Funny Girl* and *Gypsy* and such films as *Anchors Aweigh, Gentlemen Prefer Blondes,* and *Three Coins in the Fountain.*

K. T. Stevens (Vanessa Prentiss) was the daughter of film director Sam Wood, who made such classics as *Good-Bye, Mr. Chips* and the Marx Brothers comedy *A Night at the Opera.* Wood gave his daughter her first break in show business, using the two-year-old in his silent film comedy *Peck's Bad Boy,* which starred Jackie Coogan. That same year, Wood used Stevens again for another comedy, *Don't Tell Everything.* As an adult, Stevens decided to pursue an acting career and worked with her father yet again in the 1940 Ginger Rogers romance *Kitty Foyle.*

Camryn Grimes's (Cassie Newman) uncle Scott Grimes has a recurring role on the Fox drama *Party of Five* as Bailey Salinger's (Scott Wolf) best friend, Will McCorkle. It was while visiting the *Party of Five* set that Grimes decided she wanted to act.

Susan Seaforth Hayes's (JoANNA MANNING) mother, Elizabeth Harrower, was an actress herself, having worked on a number of radio soap operas. Harrower then became a head writer at *Days of Our Lives*, where Seaforth Hayes had risen to fame. Harrower received an Emmy nomination for writing *The Young and the Restless.*

Nick Benedict's (MICHAEL SCOTT) father Richard had been a television director. Among his projects, Richard Benedict had directed Eric Braeden in the TV series *The Rat Patrol.*

Michael Damian's (DANNY ROMALOTTI) father-in-law is James Best, best known to TV audiences as Deputy Enos on *The Dukes of Hazzard.*

Grant Cramer (SHAWN GARRETT and ADAM HUNTER) is the son of actress Terry Moore, who starred in a number of feature films, among them *Peyton Place* and the original *Mighty Joe Young*. In 1953, she was Oscar nominated as Best Supporting Actress for her work in *Come Back Little Sheba*. She also made a name for herself by claiming to have been secretly married to the late, reclusive billionaire Howard Hughes.

Jim Storm's (NEIL FENMORE) brother Michael is a soap actor as well, having played Dr. Larry Wolek on *One Life to Live* for the past thirty-odd years, a role which he took over from Jim Storm himself.

Peter Brown (ROBERT LAURENCE) is the uncle of Philip Brown, who played Doris Day's son on her 1960s TV series. More recently, Philip Brown has made a name for himself in soap operas. He played a record company executive on *The Colbys*, a homicidal architect on *Knots Landing*, and a reformed con artist on *Loving/The City.*

Marc Singer, who as Chet held Victor Newman hostage for weeks on end in 1999, is the brother of TV and film actress Lori Singer, best known for her work on the series *Fame* and in the 1984 Kevin Bacon movie musical *Footloose.*

Actress/singer Michelle Thomas's (CALLIE ROGERS) father Dennis played saxophone for the R&B/funk group Kool and the Gang, who recorded such dance hits as "Celebration" and "Ladies' Night."

Francesco Quinn (TOMAS DEL CERRO) is the son of Academy Award winner Anthony Quinn (*Zorba the Greek*).

Heather Tom's (VICTORIA NEWMAN) younger brother David recently joined the *Y&R* cast as Billy Abbott, Victoria's one time step uncle. (His half-brother Jack was once married to Victoria's mother Nikki.) David's twin sister Nicholle played Maggie Sheffield on the Fran Drescher sitcom *The Nanny*. When the producers were looking to age the character of Nicholas Newman, Heather Tom arranged for her younger brother David (Nicholle's twin) to be seen. She thought it would be an interesting idea for a brother and sister to be playing a brother and sister. The producers had a similar casting stunt in mind. They were hoping for Eric Braeden's son Christian to play Victor's son, but he was more interested in writing and directing.

Jeanne Cooper and her real-life son, *L.A. Law*'s Corbin Bernsen.
© *Albert Ortega, Moonglow Photos*

DAVID HASSELHOFF left his role as Dr. Snapper Foster in the early 1980s to join the cast of *Semi-Tough,* an ABC sitcom based on the Burt Reynolds film. The series was canceled after only a month, and Hasselhoff headed back to Y&R for another two years. The next time he left the show, he landed in *Knight Rider,* costarring alongside a talking car. That series lasted four years and made Hasselhoff a TV star. His next project, *Baywatch,* survived only a year in its initial stint on NBC, but went on to become enormously successful when resurrected as a syndicated series.

Although he was fired from his role as Jed Andrews presumably because Bill Bell found his voice too high and squeaky, Tom Selleck recovered nicely, landing the lead role in the Hawaii-based private eye series *Magnum, P.I.* In the 1980s, Selleck parlayed his TV popularity into a number of film roles, most popular among them *Three Men and a Baby.* More recently, he costarred with Kevin Kline in the big screen comedy *In and Out.* When Selleck went up for his first primetime pilot—a series that never made it to the air—he had been advised by one of the executives to delete Y&R from his résumé, as another actor had been turned down for the role because he was thought of as a soap actor.

A recurring role on the phenomenally successful *Seinfeld* gave John O'Hurley (DR. JIM GRAINGER) a chance to show off his gift for comedy, playing Elaine's (Julia Louis Dreyfuss) boss, J. Peterman, an adventurer/clothing cataloguer. O'Hurley who has subsequently guested on *Sunset Beach*, still holds his time on *Y&R* in high regard and says he would be open for a return visit.

Like O'Hurley, Phil Morris (TYRONE JACKSON) gained a great deal of prominence from a number of guest appearances on *Seinfeld*, including the series finale. Morris played Jackie Childs, a high-powered lawyer based on O. J. Simpson attorney Johnnie Cochran. Morris has also worked on a number of different TV series and miniseries since leaving the soap—he played a news reporter on *WIOU*, a chauffeur on *Marblehead Manor*, a spy on *Mission: Impossible*, and a gangster's son in several miniseries based on the novels of Jackie Collins. Most recently he worked on *Love Boat: The Next Wave*.

Baywatch star David Hasselhoff played Dr. Snapper Foster.
© *Albert Ortega, Moonglow Photos*

Tom Selleck was fired from *Y&R* because of his voice.

© *Albert Ortega, Moonglow Photos*

Love Boat: The Next Wave also starred Heidi Mark, who played Sharon Collins prior to Sharon Case. Mark replaced Monica Potter, who lasted only two weeks in the role. Potter has since moved into feature films. Among her most prominent roles was that of Nicolas Cage's wife in the action blockbuster *Con Air.*

After Mari Jo Mason was carted away for shooting Victor Newman, Diana Barton landed a role in Lorenzo Lamas's syndicated adventure series *Air America.*

After Phillip Chancellor Sr. was killed off, Donnelly Rhodes joined the cast of the primetime soap opera spoof *Soap,* playing a soft-hearted ex-convict.

The role of Nathan "Kong" Hastings, mob enforcer turned private investigator, was originated by Forest Whitaker, who has since gained prominence both in front of and behind the camera. He has played a hostage in the Oscar-nominated *Crying Game* and John Travolta's best friend in the big hit *Phenomenon.* He has also directed such films as *Waiting to Exhale* and *Hope Floats.*

Shortly after leaving *Y&R,* Vivica A. Fox (Stephanie Simmons) played Will Smith's stripper girlfriend in the top grossing film of 1996, the science fiction adventure *Independence Day.* She has also been seen as Mr. Freeze's (Arnold Schwarzenegger) concubine in *Batman and Robin.* Her other films include *Set It Off* and *Soul Food.*

In the early 1990s, Paul Walker played Brandon Collins, who tried to win Victoria Newman's (Heather Tom) heart away from the significantly older Ryan McNeil (Scott Reeves). Although several years older, Walker is still playing teen roles and has appeared in such big screen comedies as *Meet the Deedles, Pleasantville,* and *She's All That.*

All of the actors who have played Greg Foster have gone on to roles in primetime and films. James Houghton, who originated the role, was also an original cast member on the *Dallas* spin-off, *Knots Landing.* He played record producer Kenny Ward. In the mid-'80s, Houghton played Senator

Cash Cassidy in the *Dynasty* spin-off, *The Colbys*. Brian Kerwin, who took over the role in 1976, has subsequently moved into films and primetime. Among his more prominent screen roles, he played Harvey Fierstein's bisexual lover in the adaptation of *Torch Song Trilogy* and Robin Williams's father in the Francis Ford Coppola film *Jack*. Currently, he can be seen in the Showtime sitcom *Beggars and Choosers*. Wings Hauser, the third Greg, left in 1981. Since 1982, he has made more than forty movies, most of them action adventures and horror flicks, mainly marketed direct-to-video, a fact he has joked about on talk shows. In addition to his film work, he has also recurred as a mercenary adventurer on the Fox series *Beverly Hills, 90210*. Howard McGillin, the fourth and final Greg Foster, has lent his voice to a number of animated projects. He provided the voice for Prince Derek in *The Swan Princess*, performed in the chorus of Disney's *Beauty and the Beast: One Enchanted Christmas*, and was most recently heard singing in 1999's *South Park: Bigger, Longer, and Uncut*.

When They Were Young

Match the following soap opera actors with the roles they played on *The Young and the Restless.*

1. Tony Geary
   (Luke Spencer, *General Hospital*)

2. Deidre Hall
   (Dr. Marlena Evans, *Days of Our Lives*)

3. Mark Derwin
   (Ben Davidson, *One Life to Live*)

4. Liz Keifer
   (Blake Marler, *Guiding Light*)

5. Granville Van Dusen
   (David "DV" Bordisso, *Port Charles*)

6. Kimberlin Brown
   (Dr. Rachel Locke, *Port Charles*)

7. Rodney Van Johnson
   (TC Russell, *Passions*)

8. Lauren Koslow
   (Kate Roberts, *Days of Our Lives*)

9. John McCook
   (Eric Forrester, *The Bold and the Beautiful*)

10. Darlene Conley
   (Sally Spectra, *The Bold and the Beautiful*)

(a) Angela Laurence

(b) Keith Dennison

(c) Sheila Carter

(d) Adrian Hunter

(e) Lindsey Wells

(f) Lance Prentiss

(g) Barbara Anderson

(h) George Curtis

(i) Rose DeVille

(j) Trey Stark

BEFORE THEY WERE YOUNG

Match the following current cast members with their previous soap roles.

1. Don Diamont
(BRAD CARLTON)

(a) DEBBIE SIMON, *As the World Turns*

2. Eileen Davidson
(ASHLEY ABBOTT)

(b) KIRK McCOLL, *As the World Turns*

3. Peter Bergman
(JACK ABBOTT)

(c) TRISH CLAYTON, *Days of Our Lives*

4. Sharon Case
(SHARON NEWMAN)

(d) CARLO FORENZA, *Days of Our Lives*

5. Ricky Paull Goldin
(GARY DAWSON)

(e) KELLY CAPWELL, *Santa Barbara*

6. Tricia Cast
(NINA WEBSTER McNEIL)

(f) ADAM MARSHALL, *Generations*

7. Christian LeBlanc
(MICHAEL BALDWIN)

(g) SHELLEY GRANGER, *Capitol*

8. Jess Walton
(JILL ABBOTT)

(h) DR. CLIFF WARNER, *All My Children*

9. Kristoff St. John
(NEIL WINTERS)

(i) CHRISTY DUVALL, *Santa Barbara*

10. Patty Weaver
(GINA ROMA)

(j) DEAN FRAME, *Another World*

Just for the Record

TWO YEARS before making its debut on daytime, Y&R's instrumental theme was used in the feature film *Bless the Beasts and the Children* under the title "Cotton's Theme."

In 1987, MCA Records capitalized on the number of singers Y&R counted among its cast members. Michael Damian (DANNY ROMALOTTI), Patty Weaver (GINA ROMA), Tracey E. Bregman (LAUREN FENMORE), Beth Maitland (TRACI ABBOTT), and Colleen Casey (FARREN CONNOR) all cut tracks for the label's *Young and the Restless* album.

Eleven years later, to coincide with the show's twenty-fifth anniversary, another soundtrack was released, this one featuring all instrumental tunes. Some critics complained that the song titles gave no indication as to the context in which each piece was used, information that soap fans would want. The song "Janice" was singled out by *Soap Opera Weekly*, whose reviewer noted that the soap had never featured a major character named Janice.

Michael Damian released his first single in 1981, before landing the role of Danny Romalotti. It was a remake of the Eric Carmen song "She Did It." By the end of the decade, he had his first hit single in the United States. His remake of David Essex's "Rock On" topped *Billboard*'s pop charts in 1989 and went gold. The song was helped up the charts by exposure in both the big screen teen comedy *Dream a Little Dream* and on Y&R. Damian has always been grateful to the show's producers for incorporating the song into Danny's storyline, thereby letting him perform it a number of times onscreen. In

Singer/actor Michael Damian hit the top of the pop charts.

© *Albert Ortega, Moonglow Photos*

addition to the *Dream a Little Dream* soundtrack, "Rock On" was included on Damian's 1989 album *Where Do We Go from Here*. Although "Rock On" was Damian's breakthrough single in the United States, his 1984 debut album *Love Is a Mystery* had already gone gold in his native Canada. The kickoff single from that album, "She's in a Different World," was shown regularly on Much Music, the Canadian equivalent to MTV. Two years later he released a self-titled album, and in 1987, he recorded the holiday song "Christmas Time Without You" on his family's own label. Damian also recorded the theme song to the Saturday morning sitcom *Saved by the Bell* and was included on the show's soundtrack. He has followed up *Where Do We Go from Here* with *Dreams of Summer* (1991) and *Time of the Season* (1994), which included a duet with 1960s teen idol Frankie Avalon.

Damian's onscreen sister Patty Weaver (GINA ROMA) was performing with her own brothers long before Danny and Gina sang their first duet. The daughter of a minister, Weaver sang in public for the first time at age nine, when her father, a minister, requested that she perform "Amazing Grace" before his congregation. In her teens, she and two of her brothers formed a band called Luv'd Ones. They released the single "Going Down," which became a modest hit in the 1960s. During that time, Luv'd Ones opened for such rock headliners as the Hollies, Simon and Garfunkel, and Crosby, Stills, Nash, and Young. On her own, Weaver released a number of albums before joining *Y&R*, including *As Time Goes By, Feelings, No One's Ever Seen This Side of Me,* and *Patty Weaver*. She has also released a pair of holiday singles: "Christmas Is . . ." and "White Christmas."

In the late 1970s and early '80s, David Hasselhoff (SNAPPER FOSTER) and his onscreen brother, Wings Hauser (GREG FOSTER), would sing rock-and-roll songs at shopping malls alongside *General Hospital* star Richard Dean Anderson, later known as primetime TV's MacGyver. Both Hasselhoff and Hauser parlayed their acting careers into record deals. RCA released a number of singles by Hauser, among them "Your Love Keeps Me Off the Street" and "White Boy on the Run." Hasselhoff made an even more impressive splash in the music industry—most especially in the German market. His song

"Looking for Freedom" topped the German charts the year it was released, outselling such American superstar imports as Madonna and Michael Jackson. On New Year's Eve 1989, Hasselhoff performed "Looking for Freedom" in a crane hanging over the deconstructed Berlin Wall. More recently, he released a remake of the early 1970s hit "Hooked on a Feeling." Hasselhoff can also be heard on the 1993 soundtrack to his mega-hit TV series *Baywatch*.

John McCook won his role as Lance Prentiss not merely on his looks and acting talent but also due to his ability to sing. His very first day on the show found him belting out the Cole Porter classic "It's All Right with Me." Although he has not sung as much in his current role as Eric Forrester on *The Bold and the Beautiful*, the show's immense international appeal has helped him to land an overseas record deal. Several years ago, he released the CD *John McCook Sings Bold and Beautiful Love Songs*.

Like McCook, Lauren Koslow (LINDSEY WELLS), who also worked on *B&B* for several years, used that show's international success to release an album in Egypt and Turkey.

In the late 1950s, Robert Clary (PIERRE ROULLAND) released three albums (*Meet Robert Clary, Live at the Playboy Club,* and *"Gigi" Sung by Robert Clary*) as well as a number of singles, among them: "The Night They Invented Champagne," "Heart of Paris," and "Hotter'n a Pistol." While starring on the 1960s sitcom *Hogan's Heroes,* he and his cast mates released the album *Hogan's Heroes Sing the Best of WWII.* Clary could also be heard on the soundtrack to the 1975 film *The Hindenberg.* In the past few years, he has released another trio of CDs: *Robert Clary Sings at the Jazz Bakery* (1997), *Robert Clary Sings Rodgers, Hart and Mercer* (1998), and *Robert Clary Sings Irving Berlin and Yip Harburg* (1999).

Joshua Morrow (NICHOLAS NEWMAN), who had sung in choral groups and in church, talked his good friend and former cast mate Eddie Cibrian (MATT CLARK) into forming a singing group. The two joined with Canadian singer CJ Huyer to form the pop/R&B trio 3Deep. They lifted the title to their first CD, *yes yes yes . . . no no no,* from a line in the Mike Myers comedy

Austin Powers. "Into You," the first single from *yes yes yes . . . no no no,* was released in Canada but not the United States. In addition to singing, Morrow and Cibrian wrote and produced a number of songs on the CD.

In 1997, Brenda Epperson Doumani (ASHLEY ABBOTT) released a CD titled *I've Always Known.* In addition to several ballads, Doumani included her version of the Gloria Gaynor disco classic "I Will Survive." Several songs from the CD were written by Doumani's husband, film producer Lorenzo Doumani, who included them in his big screen romance *Follow Your Heart,* in which Brenda starred. The first single from *I've Always Known* was a remake of the Carpenters' classic "Superstar." The first time Doumani sang the song in the studio, she started to cry but didn't understand exactly why. She later learned that she was recording the song in the very same studio where the late Karen Carpenter recorded the original.

In 1993, Nick Scotti (TONY VISCARDI) released the dance CD *Wake Up Everybody,* the title track of which is a remake of a hit by Harold Melvin and the Bluenotes. Most notable on the CD is the song "Get Over," which was written by Madonna and used in the Chevy Chase–Demi Moore film *Nothing but Trouble.* Madonna, who met Scotti at a birthday party for photographer Herb Ritts, not only wrote the song for him, she also provided background vocals. A number of the other tracks were written by Scotti himself.

Scott Reeves, whose role as corporate climber Ryan McNeil has only occasionally allowed him to sing and play the guitar on air, began working on a CD last summer. He has also contributed tracks to a number of soap opera–themed CDs, including the 1992 release *With Love from the Soaps,* for which Kristoff St. John (NEIL WINTERS) also recorded a song. On *A Soap Opera Christmas: Holiday Songs from Your Favorite Daytime Stars,* Reeves dueted with Diana Barton (MARI JO MASON) on the classic "Let It Snow, Let It Snow, Let It Snow."

Country singer Carlene Carter (Johnny Cash's daughter) compared her love life to *The Young and the Restless* in the chorus of her top ten country single "Every Little Thing."

Nice to See You Again

ROD ARRANTS'S first television acting job was a three-month stint playing Jeff, one of the stableboys hired to "service" Katherine Chancellor (Jeanne Cooper). Twelve years later, Arrants returned to the show as Dr. Steven Lassiter, Ashley Abbott's (Eileen Davidson) psychiatrist and eventual husband. Arrants was surprised that his former leading lady Cooper—and many of the show's long-term fans—recognized him from his days as Jeff the stableboy. Not only was he more than a decade older, but back in the 1970s, his hair had been significantly longer and he wore a mustache.

In 1989, Jeanne Cooper, who had been playing the regal Katherine Chancellor since 1973, took on a second role, a tough waitress by the name of Marge Cotrooke. When ex-con Clint Radison (James Michael Gregory) spotted Marge working in a diner, a plot was hatched. He dyed Marge's red hair blonde, gave her diction lessons, and even had her appendix removed so that she could pass for Katherine Chancellor, whom he then kidnapped. Cooper loved playing the two roles and has often expressed her wish that the writers would bring Marge back.

One of the long-ranging plot twists during Cooper's dual storyline found Marge "divorcing" Katherine's husband Rex Sterling, played by Quinn Redeker. Rex was Redeker's third role on the show. In 1979, he played Nick Reed, the father who had raped Casey (Roberta Leighton) as a child. He was killed off that same year, when he went after Nikki (Melody Thomas Scott). He later returned for a short stint as lawyer Joseph Thomas. Fifteen years after Nikki pushed Nick to his death, Redeker played his second death scene on the show when Rex was shot to death by a burglar.

During Jeanne Cooper's dual storyline, Katherine and her pregnant maid, Esther (Kate Linder), were held hostage by an older pair of criminals named Morey and Lil. Lil was played by Lilyan Chauvin, who fifteen years previously had played Marianne Roulland, the sister of Pierre Roulland (Robert Clary). In between her stints as Marianne and Lil, Chauvin had a small role as Dina Mergeron's (Marla Adams) maid.

When Lauralee Bell first worked on *Y&R*, she was eleven years old. She was an extra in an airplane scene that featured David Hasselhoff as Snapper Foster. A couple of years later, she returned to the show as

Quinn Redeker played three roles on *Y&R*.
© *Albert Ortega, Moonglow Photos*

Cricket Blair—a role intended to be short-term. Bell has been playing the role for sixteen years and counting.

From 1984 to 1986, Grant Cramer played Shawn Garrett, a disturbed fan whose obsession with Lauren Fenmore (Tracey E. Bregman) ultimately led him to bury her alive. Ten years after Shawn was written off the show, Cramer returned as a completely new character, chemist Adam Hunter. At first, Cramer distinguished Adam from Shawn by growing a mustache. Although slated for a romance with Ashley Abbott, then played by Shari Shattuck, Cramer lasted only a few months in the role.

In the early 1980s, Melinda Cordell played April Stevens's (Cynthia Eilbacher) mother, Dorothy. In the early 1990s, she returned to the show as Drucilla Barber's (Victoria Rowell) ballet teacher, Madame Chauvin.

In the early 1980s, when Katherine Chancellor (Jeanne Cooper) got involved with freedom fighter Felipe Ramirez (Victor Mohica), Anthony Peña had a small role as the man's brother. Three years later Peña returned as Nikki's Spanish tutor–turned-butler Miguel Rodriguez, the role he has played for fifteen years and counting.

Andre Khabbazi believes that his day of work as a character named Van helped him land the recurring role of Alec Moretti.

In 1990, Kelly Garrison was seen in flashbacks as the wife David Kimble (Michael Corbett) had murdered. Later that same year, she joined the cast as Hillary Lancaster, who would marry the only slightly less villainous Michael Baldwin (Christian LeBlanc).

Mary Williams was Carolyn Conwell's fourth role on the show. She came on first in 1974 when Jill Foster (Brenda Dickson) was toying with the idea of becoming a hooker. Williams played an older prostitute who gave Jill a glimpse into the life. Years later, Williams came back as an abusive mother. She later returned as the born-again Christian mother of wife beater Ron Becker (Dick DeCoit). For each turn on the show, Conwell changed her hair so that fans would not recognize her from her previous incarnations.

Two years before taking on the role of Tricia Dennison, Sabryn Genet first appeared in Genoa City as Kelly, one of Matt Clark's (Eddie Cibrian) many female admirers.

In 1995, Michael Tylo was looking at a fairly long future on *The Young and the Restless*. Not only had he signed a five-year contract with the show—the first contract of its kind—he was playing two characters: Ashley Abbott's (Brenda Epperson) husband, Blade, a photographer, and his evil twin, Rick Bladeson. Shortly after Tylo signed his contract, however, Epperson decided not to renew her own. Blade was subsequently killed off to explain Ashley's need to leave town for a while. Tylo's other alter-ego, Rick, was also written off the show.

Brooke Logan's (Katherine Kelly Lang) crossover from *The Bold and the Beautiful* to *The Young and the Restless* was the character's first visit to Genoa City, but not the actress's. Before she landed the role of Brooke Logan, Lang had spent a summer on *Y&R* as Patty Williams's (Lilibet Stern) friend Gretchen.

Similarly, longtime fans must have recognized John McCook from his days as Lance Prentiss on *Y&R* when Sheila Carter (Kimberlin Brown), who had been transplanted to *The Bold and the Beautiful,* answered Eric Forrester's want ad for a nanny.

Usually, a span of at least a few months separates an actor's unrelated stints on the show. Velekka Gray, however, played both Dr. Sharon Reaves and Ruby, a manicurist, during the same stretch of time.

Just Passing Through Town

A **YEAR AFTER** winning her Olympic gold medal, figure skater Tara Lipinski fulfilled another dream by guest-starring on her favorite soap, *The Young and the Restless*. The appearance was one of the perks in a contract she signed with CBS to star in her own skating special. Lipinski's guest shot as Megan Dennison's (Ashley Jones) friend Marnie impressed *Y&R*'s producers so much that they have brought her back several times.

In the early 1980s, another celebrity fan made his debut on the show. Hockey great Wayne Gretzky filmed a cameo as a well-dressed mobster. As much as he enjoyed the experience, he saw it as a one-time gig. He has turned down guest appearance offers from other soap operas, including those he watches.

Several other professional athletes have also appeared on the show. Retired baseball great Steve Garvey played a business acquaintance of John Abbott (Jerry Douglas). Atlanta Brave Dave Justice played an associate of Victor Newman's (Eric Braeden). Flipper Anderson of the Los Angeles Rams pushed a wheelchair down the corridor during a hospital scene.

Phyllis Romalotti's (Michelle Stafford) mother, Lydia, was portrayed by Abby Dalton, who played the villainous Julia Cumson on the primetime serial *Falcon Crest* for many years.

When the decision was made to flesh out Victor Newman's (Eric Braeden) past by introducing the mother who had given him up at birth, the producers wanted an actress of some prominence to fill the role of Cora Miller. Fitting that bill was longtime Hollywood leading lady Dorothy McGuire, who had been Oscar nominated as Best Actress for her role in the 1947 Elia Kazan drama *Gentleman's Agreement*. Among her other notable films are *A Tree Grows in Brooklyn*, *Three Coins in the Fountain*, and *Old Yeller*. On TV, she had been Emmy nominated for her work in the miniseries *Rich Man, Poor Man*.

When Jill Abbott (Jess Walton) was arrested for the attempted murder of Victor Newman, the judge presiding over her case was played by Isabel Sanford, best known to primetime audiences as Louise ("Weezy") Jefferson on the long-running CBS sitcom *The Jeffersons*.

Celebrity impersonator Rich Little played himself during the storyline in which Brad Carlton (Don Diamont) was kidnapped by his deranged ex-wife, Lisa Mansfield (Lynn Harbaugh). Lisa tricked Little into impersonating Brad's voice on a pair of tape-recorded good-byes, one for Brad's wife Traci (Beth Maitland), the other for his boss and sometimes lover Lauren Fenmore (Tracey E. Bregman). Head writer Bill Bell felt that Little, who was famous for his vocal impersonations, lent the plot twist a greater level of credibility.

Talk-show host Geraldo Rivera appeared as himself during a restaurant scene. Rivera recognized Traci Abbott (Beth Maitland) as a famous writer and invited her to be a guest on his show.

The 1986 summer storyline in which rocker Danny Romalotti (Michael Damian) examined the connection between pop music and teen pregnancy ended with a concert promoting the message that it was "okay to say no." In addition to Damian and varied cast members, the concert included a performance by former Doobie Brother Michael McDonald. McDonald sang a number of songs including "Sweet Freedom," which had been a top ten hit that summer.

Star power alone is not enough to land a celebrity fan on the show, and Bill Bell would not let any guest star dictate their own terms. Queen of

Soul Aretha Franklin had long expressed an interest in appearing on the show. During the 1986 teen pregnancy storyline, Bell came up with a character he thought would have been perfect for Franklin; he wanted her to play the mother of a pregnant teen. Franklin, however, wasn't interested in that role. She wanted something more fun, something that would have her mixing it up with her favorite characters, Victor and Nikki. Bell didn't see that working out, and Franklin has yet to appear on the show.

$\mathcal{F}$amous $\mathcal{F}$ans

AFTER ONE particularly hard day on the set, Melody Thomas Scott (NIKKI NEWMAN) was in no mood to be recognized. While reading through a soap magazine at a newsstand, she was interrupted by a tap on the shoulder. When the fan asked if she was indeed Melody Thomas, the actress nodded but kept her face buried inside the magazine. Thomas Scott didn't lift her head until the woman introduced herself as Aretha Franklin. Franklin, who watches the entire CBS lineup, will not allow people to disturb her in the afternoons until after her soaps have ended.

Recently retired hockey great Wayne Gretzky has been watching *The Young and the Restless* for twenty-two years. When he joined the Los Angeles Kings and moved into his California home, he had a TV with satellite feed hooked up in his gym, allowing him to watch East Coast transmissions of *Y&R*, *One Life to Live*, and *General Hospital* during his morning workouts. Gretzky counts sports fanatic and *Y&R* star Joshua Morrow (NICHOLAS NEWMAN) among his good friends.

Back in the mid-1980s, Michael Damian's (DANNY ROMALOTTI) busy schedule as an actor and singer kept him from attending a Lionel Richie concert. After finishing up his work for the night, Damian headed out to a bar with a friend. While the two were sitting there, they were surprised to be approached by Lionel Richie, who introduced himself to Damian. Richie, a big fan of *The Young and the Restless,* asked if he could join Damian and his friend for a drink. During Richie's recent European concert tour, Brenda Epperson Doumani (the former ASHLEY ABBOTT) opened for him.

Anthony Stewart Head, who plays mentor to Sarah Michelle Gellar on *Buffy the Vampire Slayer*, watches *The Young and the Restless* from his studio trailer.

John Henton, star of the ABC sitcom *The Hughleys*, watches both *All My Children* and *The Young and the Restless*. When Henton lived in New York, this required flipping back and forth between the two shows during the half hour they overlap in Eastern time zones.

Fran Drescher, who starred in *The Nanny*, got to work with some of her *Y&R* favorites, including Eric Braeden (VICTOR NEWMAN) and Shemar Moore (MALCOLM WINTERS), when they guest-starred on her sitcom. One episode found Drescher's character Fran landing a role on *Y&R*, which featured Peter Bergman playing himself. In the plot, Fran could not seem to get through a kissing scene with him and was subsequently fired.

Anti-feminist writer Camille Paglia (author of *Sexual Personae*) has been watching *Y&R* since its debut. She will often take notes on the show, as well as other soap operas, for her books and essays on pop culture. She once picked Nikki Newman as the ideal female soap heroine.

Soul singer Isaac Hayes hit number one on *Billboard*'s Hot 100 with the theme from *Shaft*. In the past few years, he has enjoyed a career resurgence. Among his recent endeavors, he provides the voice of Chef on Comedy Central's animated hit *South Park*. A self-confessed fan of the entire CBS daytime lineup, Hayes introduced a segment on soap opera enemies at the 1999 Soap Opera Awards. He has also invited a number of *Y&R* cast members to appear on his New York–based radio show. During Siena Goines's (CALLIE ROGERS) appearance, the two dueted on an impromptu version of "It's Too Late Baby."

While Eric Braeden (VICTOR NEWMAN) was driving home one night, a white Rolls Royce pulled up beside him. "Victor, my man," came a voice from the limo's backseat. Taking a closer look, Braeden recognized the passenger as boxer Tommy Hearns, who offered Braeden help in dealing with all of Victor's ladies.

Other professional boxers who tune in regularly include George Foreman, who has visited the Y&R set, and Sugar Ray Leonard, whom Braeden considers a personal friend.

A number of baseball players also follow the show. While travelling on the road, Baltimore Oriole Cal Ripken Jr. checks into hotels under the name Brad Carlton. New York Mets catcher Mike Piazza picked up his Y&R habit from his mother. New York Yankee Danny Tartabull, who has been

Victor Newman (Eric Braeden) is a favorite among sports stars.
© Albert Ortega, Moonglow Photos

watching since 1984, uses the show's theme song as his makeshift alarm clock. When he hears it playing, he knows that it's time to get out of bed.

Angela Cartwright, best known as Penny Robinson on the 1960s science fiction series *Lost in Space*, plays mah-jong with Peter Bergman's (JACK ABBOTT) wife, Mariellen. Occasionally Mariellen will fill Cartwright in on upcoming storyline twists.

Nichelle Nichols, who played Lieutenant Uhura on the original *Star Trek* series, makes up her own nicknames for the different characters. For instance, she calls Katherine Chancellor (Jeanne Cooper) "Rich Rocks."

Toni Braxton, who has recorded such hit singles as "Breathe Again" and "Un-Break My Heart," specifically requested Shemar Moore (MALCOLM WINTERS) to appear in the video for her song "How Many Ways."

Similarly, pop singer Richard Marx, who has recorded such hit singles as "It Don't Mean Nothing" and "Hold Onto the Night," recruited Lauralee Bell (CHRISTINE WILLIAMS) for a role in the video for his song "Until I Find You Again." The video, set in an old movie theater, cast Bell as a woman from the 1940s. It was her first music video.

Barry Gibb, whose group the Bee Gees recorded such disco classics as "Night Fever" and "Stayin' Alive," once talked to the producers about guesting on the show either as himself or in character.

Vince Neal, former lead singer for the rock group Motley Crue, has been watching Y&R since he was a child. When his former girlfriend Heidi Mark was playing Sharon Collins, he would let her know what he thought of her scenes and of the show in general.

David Robinson, who played drums for the rock group the Cars ("Drive," "You Might Think"), admired Terry Lester's portrayal of Jack Abbott as the show's leading bad boy.

When Donny and Marie Osmond welcomed a number of actors from Y&R to their daytime talk show, Marie admitted that she has from time to time followed the show. When she was eighteen, the highly religious Marie confessed to *People* magazine that she felt guilty for having gotten hooked on a soap opera for two weeks.

At the 1998 Winter Olympics, Tara Lipinski became the youngest figure skater to win a gold medal. That same year, she visited the *Y&R* set, where she met Eric Braeden, Melody Thomas Scott, and Sandra Nelson (PHYLLIS ROMALOTTI). Although in her early teens, Lipinski was already a loyal fan of the show. While training for the Olympics, she would unwind between sessions by watching *Y&R* with her mother.

Tennis great John McEnroe admitted he was a *Y&R* fan while competing in the U.S. Open. The camera panned to Susan Lucci (ERICA KANE, *All My Children*) sitting in the stands, to which McEnroe remarked that one day he wanted to see Erica go head-to-head with Victor Newman.

A former gymnast, Sabryn Genet (TRICIA DENNISON) was excited to see 1976 gold medalist Nadia Comaneci and her husband, gymnast Bart Connors, at a function honoring professional athletes. Although Genet wanted to meet the pair, she was discouraged from doing so by the sheer number of people surrounding them. A little while later, someone tapped her on the shoulder and apologized for bothering her, but explained "my wife wants to meet you." The man was Bart Connors. Genet learned that Comaneci, who performed to the theme from *Y&R* at the Montreal Olympics, had since become a fan of the show.

Esther Williams, the champion swimmer who starred in such Hollywood musicals as *Bathing Beauty*, *Neptune's Daughter*, and *Million Dollar Mermaid*, ran into Roberta Leighton (DR. CASEY REED) at a Hollywood function in the late 1980s. During the meeting, Williams admonished Leighton for the way Casey was treating her sister Nikki.

Former Houston Oiler wide receiver Haywood Jeffries has gotten so riled up at the happenings in Genoa City—usually those caused by Victor Newman—that he has literally broken his TV set more than a dozen times. It was not uncommon for him to throw his glass right at the screen. In a 1995 article in *Sports Illustrated*, he blamed Victor Newman for more than ˙$6,000 worth of damage.

Even before Patti D'Arbanville joined the cast of *Guiding Light*, she was a daytime fan. The 1999 Daytime Emmy Awards gave her a chance to meet one of her favorites, Jess Walton (JILL ABBOTT), who turned out to be a fan of D'Arbanville's work as well. As soon as the two spotted each other, they began gushing about how much they admired each other's work.

Royal fan Prince Albert of Monaco invited both Lauralee Bell (CHRISTINE WILLIAMS) and Michael Damian (DANNY ROMALOTTI) to the palace when he learned that they were vacationing in Monte Carlo. Rumors immediately spread that Prince Albert planned to marry Bell the way his father had married American actress Grace Kelly.

Cast Members Who Were Fans First

THE LATE Michelle Thomas (CALLIE ROGERS) considered herself very lucky when she landed the role of Urkel's (Jaleel White) girlfriend Myra on *Family Matters*, which was her favorite sitcom. As that show was winding down, her agent asked whether Thomas was interested in doing a soap opera. Thomas had always wanted to work on one, specifically on *The Young and the Restless*, which she had been watching for years. She picked up the habit from her mother, who had been following the show from the very first episode.

Current headwriter Kay Alden first started watching *The Young and the Restless* as research for a dissertation she was writing on daytime serials as mediators of social change. As part of her research, she travelled from Madison, Wisconsin, where she was attending the University of Wisconsin, to Chicago to interview the show's creator, Bill Bell. Toward the end of that interview, she wound up with more than a nice set of quotes—she had found a mentor. Bell invited her to submit some sample scripts and eventually took her on as a writer.

Katherine Kelly Lang (BROOKE LOGAN, *The Bold and the Beautiful*) was hooked on *Y&R* when she was in her late teens and early twenties. Although she spent a summer recurring as Patty Williams's friend Gretchen, she was not interested in signing a long-term contract.

Gene Anthony Ray, who played dancer Leroy Johnson in the film and TV series *Fame*, was long acquainted with the denizens of Genoa City by the time he was hired to choreograph the dance scenes between Heather Tom (VICTORIA NEWMAN) and Nick Scotti (TONY VISCARDI).

When Barbara Crampton (LEANNE LOVE) was growing up, she would hurry home from school to watch *The Young and the Restless* with her sisters.

Even as a child, Sabryn Genet (TRICIA DENNISON) preferred soap operas to cartoons. She was initially drawn to *The Young and the Restless* because of the opening music. As a gymnast, Genet recognized the show's theme song from Romanian gymnast Nadia Comaneci's gold-winning program.

When Dealing with the Public

BACK IN the days before most viewers knew soap opera actors by their real names, David Hasselhoff would make personal appearances and fans would simply shout out his character's name: "Snapper! Snapper!" Hasselhoff would of course use his real name when signing autographs. One woman looked at the name he'd written, looked back at him, and asked, "David *What?*"

Tracey E. Bregman had a terrifying encounter with one fan who obviously didn't take too kindly to Lauren Fenmore's various machinations. The young man pulled his car up beside her own and began honking his horn and shouting at her. He then cut in front of her several times and slammed on his brakes. When Bregman tried to drive away, he followed her. At one point, he got out of his car to accost her. The chase lasted almost an hour, after which she finally managed to lose him.

One fan tried a rather unusual approach to getting Eric Braeden's (VICTOR NEWMAN) attention at a party. She dumped her drink onto his pants.

One Scott Reeves (RYAN MCNEIL) fan slipped into the *Y&R* studio, found Reeves's dressing room, shut the door, and started watching television with the actor as though there was nothing amiss.

While heading off to a personal appearance in Canada, Thom Bierdz (PHILLIP CHANCELLOR III) had his pocket picked. In addition to Bierdz's wallet, the thief had made off with his passport as well, which could have made it difficult for the actor to get into Canada. Luckily for Bierdz, two

Tracey E. Bregman (pictured here with Victoria Rowell and
Lauralee Bell) was chased home by one disturbed fan.

© *Albert Ortega, Moonglow Photos*

of the young women working at customs recognized him from Y&R and allowed him through without identification. He did, however, have trouble getting back into the United States. In lieu of a passport or drivers license, he was able to use a soap opera magazine, which happened to feature him on the cover that week.

A group of young fans who often followed Bierdz home from the studio became such a nuisance not only for himself but for his landlady that he was forced to move into a high-security building.

Kate Linder's second job as a flight attendant allowed her a number of encounters with the show's fans. Two young women, who knew of Linder's second career, were disappointed to find that Linder was not working the day of their flight. They did, however, request the autograph of another attendant simply because she knew Linder. Two other fans were so excited to see Linder in the airport that they followed her onto the plane only to then realize that they belonged on another flight. One time, Linder would have much preferred not to have been recognized. Shortly after takeoff, her plane turned right around and headed back to the airport. One of the passengers, it turned out, was transporting drugs. As the drug dealer was being led away by federal agents, he looked at Linder and asked, "Aren't you Esther on *The Young and the Restless?*"

One of the best looking sets on Y&R is the Chancellor mansion. The living room set always looks so immaculate that Kate Linder has received mail from fans wanting to know what specific brands of cleaning products Esther uses.

Melissa Morgan, who played attorney Brittany Norman, received a number of letters from prison inmates asking her to represent them in their appeals.

While having a drink with her sister, Tamara Clatterbuck (ALICE JOHNSON) was approached by an off-duty firefighter, who informed her that *The Young and the Restless* was a big hit back in his firehouse. A few minutes after he excused himself to make a phone call, an entire truck full of firefighters in uniform showed up, wanting to meet Clatterbuck.

A traffic officer who helped Laura Bryan Birn (LYNNE BASSETT) cross the street asked for her autograph. Because neither had a piece of paper handy, Birn signed the inside of his hat.

Heather Tom (VICTORIA NEWMAN) once autographed a fan's shaved head.

Signy Coleman's portrayal of blind farm owner Hope Adams convinced more than a few fans that Coleman herself was blind. She amazed one such fan when she drove into a car dealership. As soon as the woman spotted Coleman getting out of the driver's side of her truck, she began yelling that it was "a miracle."

Heather Tom was disconcerted by the amount of negative backlash when Victoria began an interracial romance with Neil Winters (Kristoff St. John). Even people who claimed they were not prejudiced wrote to tell her that they didn't like the idea of the relationship. While fans wrote to Tom to express their disapproval, others literally sent death threats to St. John.

For one fan, *The Young and the Restless* has been more than a source of entertainment. In one episode, baby Nicholas Newman accidentally swallowed a dime and required infant CPR. His father, Victor, performed the procedure. The day after that episode aired, one grateful viewer called up to say that she had seen the show and had imitated Victor's actions that same day to save her own baby.

And the Emmy Goes to . . .

LESS THAN a year after its debut, *The Young and the Restless* won its first pair of Emmys, for art direction/scenic design and lighting. A year later, it walked away with the grand prize, Best Daytime Drama. Although the show suffered a nomination drought in the early 1980s and its actors were barely acknowledged until the '90s, *The Young and the Restless* has racked up an impressive sixty-nine Daytime Emmys, more than any other soap opera. It is, in fact, second only to *Sesame Street* in terms of Daytime Emmy wins. (For the sake of space, only the winners from the technical categories are mentioned here.)

THE 1974 DAYTIME EMMY AWARDS

Many critics found it appropriate that *The Young and the Restless* should win its first Emmys for its design and lighting. The show, with its dim, movie-style lighting and its elaborate sets, had literally changed the way daytime looked.

Emmys

Outstanding Art Direction or Scenic Design

Outstanding Lighting Direction

THE 1975 DAYTIME EMMY AWARDS

Barely two years after its first episode, *The Young and the Restless* walked away with the Emmy for Outstanding Daytime Drama Series—quite a feat when you consider that such soap opera veterans as *Guiding Light, As the World Turns,* and *Search for Tomorrow* had never been nominated for the award. Bill Bell, who was headwriting both *Y&R* and *Days of Our Lives* competed against himself for the writing award. Although the odds were two to one in his favor of going home a winner, he lost out to the only other nominee in the category, the writing staff from *Another World.*

Emmys
Outstanding Daytime Drama Series

Outstanding Individual Director: Richard Dunlap

Nominations
Outstanding Writing

THE 1976 DAYTIME EMMY AWARDS

Once again, Bill Bell competed against himself for the writing award. This year, he won for *Days.*

Nominations
Outstanding Daytime Drama

Outstanding Individual Director: Richard Dunlap

Outstanding Writing

THE 1978 DAYTIME EMMY AWARDS

After being shut out of the nominations in 1977, *Y&R* bounced back with two victories. Richard Dunlap picked up his second Emmy for direction. The year also saw the return of Emmys for technical achievement, which has long been a strong suit for *Y&R.*

Emmys
Outstanding Individual Director: Richard Dunlap

Outstanding Individual Achievement in
Daytime Programming: Camera Operators

Nominations

Outstanding Daytime Series

THE 1979 DAYTIME EMMY AWARDS

The directing category was changed, no longer presented to individuals but to teams. As such, two-time winner Richard Dunlap shared his nomination with Bill Glenn.

Nominations

Outstanding Daytime Drama
Outstanding Direction
Outstanding Writing

THE 1983 DAYTIME EMMY AWARDS

After a particularly long dry spell, during which ABC dominated the Emmys, *The Young and the Restless* came back strong, picking up its second Emmy as Outstanding Daytime Drama Series. Making the victory all the more impressive, *Y&R* won the Best Show Emmy without so much as being nominated for a single other award in the acting, writing, or directing categories—a trick that has only been pulled off three times in Daytime Emmy history.

Emmys

Outstanding Daytime Drama Series

THE 1984 DAYTIME EMMY AWARDS

Terry Lester, who had been playing the ruthless Jack Abbott since 1980, picked up *Y&R*'s first acting nomination—the only major Emmy nomination the show would receive this year. Lester might very well have known going into the ceremony that he would be leaving empty-handed. In one of the Emmy's most embarrassing moments, the names of the winners had been released to the press in advance of the ceremony, which was held for the first time at night but not televised. Although most publications held the story back, an afternoon edition of *The New York Post* enjoyed a scoop by announcing the winners ahead of the ceremony.

Nominations
Outstanding Actor: Terry Lester (JACK ABBOTT)

THE 1985 DAYTIME EMMY AWARDS

The Young and the Restless picked up its third Best Show Emmy ten years after winning its first. Making the occasion extra special, the show's actors were finally winning awards. Beth Maitland (TRACI ABBOTT) and Tracey E. Bregman (LAUREN FENMORE), whose characters had been battling it out onscreen for years, were placed into separate acting categories, and each went home a winner. Maitland won for Best Supporting Actress while Bregman picked up the first Emmy ever presented for Best Ingenue—an ironically named category because no one would have described the scheming Lauren Fenmore as "unworldly."

Emmys
Oustanding Daytime Drama Series

Outstanding Supporting Actress: Beth Maitland (TRACI ABBOTT)

Outstanding Ingenue: Tracey E. Bregman (LAUREN FENMORE)

Outstanding Achievement for a Technical Team

Outstanding Achievement in Make-up

Nominations
Outstanding Actor: Terry Lester (JACK ABBOTT)

Outstanding Writing

The 1986 Daytime Emmy Awards

The Young and the Restless picked up its second Best Show Emmy in a row, its fourth overall. It also picked up the award for Outstanding Direction and *temporarily* the award for Outstanding Writing. In what has to be the most embarrassing oversight in Daytime Emmy history, the wrong name was written on the card inside the envelope. Although the writing award was supposed to go to the crew from *Guiding Light, The Young and the Restless* was announced as the winner. The very next morning, producer/headwriter Bill Bell got a phone call breaking the bad news. It would have been the first Emmy that Bell received for writing *Y&R*.

Emmys
Outstanding Drama Series

Outstanding Direction

Outstanding Videotape Editing

Outstanding Live and Tape Sound Mixing and Sound Effects

Nominations
Outstanding Actor: Terry Lester (JACK ABBOTT)

Outstanding Writing

The 1987 Daytime Emmy Awards

Eric Braeden and Terry Lester, who played onscreen rivals Victor Newman and Jack Abbott, competed against each other in the Lead Actor category.

Emmys
Outstanding Direction

Outstanding Art Direction/Set Decoration/Scenic Design

Outstanding Costume Design

Outstanding Technical Direction/Electronic Camera/Video Control

Outstanding Live and Tape Sound Mixing and Sound Effects

Outstanding Daytime Drama Series

Outstanding Lead Actor:
Eric Braeden (VICTOR NEWMAN) and Terry Lester (JACK ABBOTT)

Outstanding Ingenue: Tracey E. Bregman (LAUREN FENMORE)

Outstanding Writing

THE 1988 DAYTIME EMMY AWARDS

The Young and the Restless proved its dominance yet again in direction, picking up its fifth Emmy in the category.

Emmys

Outstanding Direction

Outstanding Videotape Editing

Outstanding Live and Tape Sound Mixing and Sound Effects

Nominations

Outstanding Drama Series

THE 1989 DAYTIME EMMY AWARDS

Jeanne Cooper, who had been playing Katherine Chancellor since the show's first year on the air, picked up her first Daytime Emmy nomination—for Best Actress. Her leading man, Quinn Redeker (REX STERLING) was nominated as Supporting Actor, one of those occasions when members of soap couple are nominated in uneven categories.

Emmys

Outstanding Directing Team

Outstanding Musical Direction and Composition

Outstanding Art Direction/Set Decoration/Scenic Design

Outstanding Videotape Editing

Outstanding Live and Tape Sound Mixing and Sound Effects

Nominations
Outstanding Drama Series

Outstanding Lead Actress: Jeanne Cooper (KATHERINE CHANCELLOR)

Outstanding Supporting Actor: Quinn Redeker (REX STERLING)

THE 1990 DAYTIME EMMY AWARDS

Once again, Jack Abbott and Victor Newman were duking it out for Best
Actor. This time, however, there was a new Jack Abbott. Peter Bergman's
Best Actor nomination was an Emmy rarity twice over: Bergman became
one of the few actors who have been nominated for two different roles on
daytime, having been nominated previously for his portrayal of Cliff
Warner on *All My Children;* Jack Abbott, in turn, became one of the few
roles to earn Emmy nominations for two different actors.

Emmys
Outstanding Make-up

Outstanding Technical Direction/Electronic Camera/Video Control

Outstanding Videotape Editing

Outstanding Live and Tape Sound Mixing and Sound Effects

Nominations
Outstanding Daytime Drama Series

Outstanding Lead Actor:
Eric Braeden (VICTOR NEWMAN) and Peter Bergman (JACK ABBOTT)

Outstanding Lead Actress: Jeanne Cooper (KATHERINE CHANCELLOR)

Outstanding Supporting Actor: Quinn Redeker (REX STERLING)

Outstanding Supporting Actress: Jess Walton (JILL ABBOTT)

Outstanding Direction

Outstanding Writing

THE 1991 DAYTIME EMMY AWARDS

In his second year as Jack Abbott, Peter Bergman was named Best Actor. Jess Walton, also a recast, picked up her first Emmy. Tricia Cast (NINA WEBSTER) lost the Best Younger Actress Emmy to future movie star Anne Heche, who was playing twins on *Another World*.

Emmys

Outstanding Lead Actor: Peter Bergman (JACK ABBOTT)

Outstanding Supporting Actress: Jess Walton (JILL ABBOTT)

Outstanding Technical Direction/Electronic Camera/Video Control

Outstanding Videotape Editing

Outstanding Live and Tape Sound Mixing and Sound Effects

Nominations

Outstanding Daytime Drama Series

Outstanding Lead Actress: Jeanne Cooper (KATHERINE CHANCELLOR)

Outstanding Younger Actress: Tricia Cast (NINA WEBSTER)

Outstanding Direction

Outstanding Writing

THE 1992 DAYTIME EMMY AWARDS

This year belonged to *The Young and the Restless*. Bill Bell, who created the series and served not only as its head writer but also as an executive producer, was awarded a Lifetime Achievement Award for his contributions to daytime. Appropriately timed, he also finally won his first Emmy for writing *Y&R*. During his acceptance speech, he recalled the mishap from

Two-time best actor Peter Bergman never forgets
to thank his wife Mariellen.

© *Albert Ortega, Moonglow Photos*

1986, then joked to the crowd that if his phone rang the next morning, he had no intention of answering it.

Peter Bergman pulled off another coup for the show, winning his second Best Actor Emmy in a row, a feat which placed him into an elite category. Kristoff St. John also pulled off a trick rarely accomplished on daytime— he received an Emmy award for his first year's work on the show. One year earlier, he had been nominated in the same category for his work on *Generations*. Among the actresses Tricia Cast beat out for her Younger Actress Emmy was Melissa Reeves (JENNIFER HORTON, *Days of Our Lives*), the real-life wife of her leading man, Scott Reeves (RYAN MCNEIL). Cast had originally worried that her ninety-minute reel was too long and would annoy the judges.

Emmys

Outstanding Lead Actor: Peter Bergman (JACK ABBOTT)

Outstanding Younger Actor: Kristoff St. John (NEIL WINTERS)

Outstanding Younger Actress: Tricia Cast (NINA WEBSTER)

Outstanding Writing Team

Outstanding Mulitple Camera Editing

Outstanding Live and Tape Sound Mixing and Sound Effects

Nominations

Outstanding Daytime Drama Series

Outstanding Lead Actress: Jeanne Cooper (KATHERINE CHANCELLOR)

Outstanding Directing Team

THE 1993 DAYTIME EMMY AWARDS

The Young and the Restless won a record-breaking fifth Emmy as Outstanding Daytime Drama. Kimberlin Brown, whose villainous Sheila Carter had been transplanted to *B&B,* received a supporting actress nomination for her work on *Y&R* even though the character had spent the lion's share of the eligibility period on *B&B.*

Emmys

Outstanding Daytime Drama

Outstanding Younger Actress: Heather Tom (VICTORIA NEWMAN)

Outstanding Costume Design
(tied with *The Bold and the Beautiful*)

Outstanding Technical Direction/Electronic Camera/Video Control

Outstanding Live and Tape Sound Mixing and Sound Effects

Nominations

Outstanding Lead Actor: Peter Bergman (JACK ABBOTT)

Outstanding Supporting Actress: Kimberlin Brown (SHEILA CARTER)

Outstanding Younger Actor: Kristoff St. John (NEIL WINTERS)

Outstanding Directing Team

Outstanding Writing Team

THE 1994 DAYTIME EMMY AWARDS

Best actor nominee Peter Bergman co-hosted the ceremony alongside former castmate Susan Lucci (ERICA KANE, *All My Children*) as well as actors from *One Life to Live* and *Days of Our Lives*. *The Young and the Restless* took home only one award, which it had to share, tying with *B&B* for Outstanding Lighting Direction.

Emmys

Outstanding Lighting Direction
(tied with *The Bold and the Beautiful*)

Nominations

Outstanding Daytime Drama Series

Outstanding Lead Actor: Peter Bergman (JACK ABBOTT)

Outstanding Supporting Actress: Signy Coleman (HOPE ADAMS)

Outstanding Younger Actress: Heather Tom (VICTORIA NEWMAN)

Outstanding Directing Team

Outstanding Writing Team

THE 1995 DAYTIME EMMY AWARDS

For the second year in a row, *The Young and the Restless* had to split its one victory with another show. This time, *Y&R* tied with *One Life to Live* for the Outstanding Art Direction/Set Decoration/Scenic Design Emmy.

Emmys
Outstanding Art Direction/Set Decoration/Scenic Design
(tied with *One Life to Live*)

Nominations
Outstanding Daytime Drama

Outstanding Lead Actor: Peter Bergman (JACK ABBOTT)

Outstanding Younger Actress: Heather Tom (VICTORIA NEWMAN)

Outstanding Directing Team

Outstanding Writing Team

THE 1996 DAYTIME EMMY AWARDS

CBS used this year's awards ceremony to heavily promote *The Young and the Restless*. Eric Braeden and Melody Thomas Scott, who play the show's reigning supercouple Victor Newman and Nikki Reed, co-hosted the festivities. As a lead-in for the ceremony, CBS broadcast a special primetime epsiode of *Y&R*, in which both Nikki and Victor were prominently featured. Nikki was preparing to marry Brad Carlton (Don Diamont) as Victor was shot in the back by an unseen assailant. The Best Supporting Actress category found three performers from the show competing against one another—an Emmy rarity not seen since the early 1980s.

Emmys
Outstanding Directing Team

Nominations
Outstanding Daytime Drama

Outstanding Lead Actor:
Peter Bergman (JACK ABBOTT) and Eric Braeden (VICTOR NEWMAN)

Outstanding Lead Actress: Jess Walton (JILL ABBOTT)

Outstanding Supporting Actress:
Victoria Rowell (DRUCILLA WINTERS); Michelle Stafford (PHYLLIS ROMALOTTI); and Tonya Lee Williams (DR. OLIVIA BARBER)

Outstanding Younger Actor:
Joshua Morrow (NICHOLAS NEWMAN) and Shemar Moore (MALCOLM WINTERS)

Outstanding Younger Actress:
Sharon Case (SHARON NEWMAN) and Heather Tom (VICTORIA NEWMAN)

Outstanding Writing Team

THE 1997 DAYTIME EMMY AWARDS

Jess Walton became one of only a handful of performers to win Emmys in both the lead and supporting categories for the same role. Michelle Stafford, who had left the show several months before to star on Aaron Spelling's new primetime serial *Pacific Palisades,* picked up the award for Supporting Actress. *The Young and the Restless* tied with *All My Children* for one of the evening's biggest awards, Outstanding Writing Team, the first time there had ever been a tie in the writing category.

Emmys
Outstanding Lead Actress: Jess Walton (JILL ABBOTT)

Outstanding Supporting Actress: Michelle Stafford (PHYLLIS ROMALOTTI)

Outstanding Directing Team

Jess Walton
has won
Emmy Awards as
Best Actress and
Best Supporting
Actress.
© Albert Ortega,
Moonglow Photos

Outstanding Writing Team (tied with *All My Children*)

Outstanding Art Direction/Set Decoration/Scenic Design
(tied with *Days of Our Lives*)

Outstanding Technical Direction/Electronic Camera/Video Control

Outstanding Lighting Direction

Nominations

Outstanding Daytime Drama

Outstanding Lead Actor:
Peter Bergman (JACK ABBOTT) and Eric Braeden (VICTOR NEWMAN)

Outstanding Supporting Actor:
Aaron Lustig (DR. TIM REID) and Scott Reeves (RYAN MCNEIL)

Outstanding Supporting Actress: Victoria Rowell (DRUCILLA WINTERS)

Outstanding Younger Actor:
Shemar Moore (MALCOLM WINTERS) and Joshua Morrow (NICHOLAS NEWMAN)

Outstanding Younger Actress:
Sharon Case (SHARON NEWMAN) and Heather Tom (VICTORIA NEWMAN)

THE 1998 DAYTIME EMMY AWARDS

Eric Braeden (VICTOR NEWMAN) won the award for Outstanding Lead Actor but did not attend the awards ceremony. Although he maintains that a prior commitment kept him from making the trek from Los Angeles to New York, *TV Guide* columnist Michael Logan reported that Braeden stayed in Los Angeles because he was unhappy with the travel arrangements made for him. Braeden received his Emmy on the *Y&R* set when Melody Thomas Scott surprised him with it during a scene. Scott Reeves (RYAN MCNEIL) was beaten out of the Supporting Actor trophy by *General Hospital*'s Steve Burton, whom Reeves had beaten out years before for the role of Ryan. Kristoff St. John wrote, produced, and directed a video documentary on the year's Emmy ceremony.

Emmys

Outstanding Lead Actor: Eric Braeden (VICTOR NEWMAN)

Outstanding Directing Team

Outstanding Art Direction/Set Decoration/Scenic Design

Outstanding Technical Direction/Electronic Camera/Video Control

Nominations

Outstanding Drama Series

Outstanding Lead Actor: Peter Bergman (JACK ABBOTT)

Outstanding Supporting Actor: Scott Reeves (RYAN MCNEIL)

Outstanding Supporting Actress: Victoria Rowell (DRUCILLA WINTERS)

Outstanding Younger Actor:
Josh Morrow (NICHOLAS NEWMAN)
and Bryant Jones (NATHAN HASTINGS)

Outstanding Younger Actress:
Heather Tom (VICTORIA NEWMAN)
and Camryn Grimes (CASSIE NEWMAN)

Outstanding Writing Team

THE 1999 DAYTIME EMMY AWARDS

The Young and the Restless earned a record setting twenty-one Daytime Emmy nominations. In almost all of the acting categories, at least two performers from the show were nominated. Heather Tom (VICTORIA NEWMAN), who won her second Emmy as Outstanding Younger Actress, found herself competing against two cast mates: Ashley Jones (MEGAN DENNISON) and Camryn Grimes (CASSIE NEWMAN). Twenty-year veteran Melody Thomas Scott (NIKKI NEWMAN), who once jokingly referred to herself as "the non-nominated Susan Lucci," received her very first Emmy nod.

Emmys

Outstanding Supporting Actress: Sharon Case (SHARON NEWMAN)

Outstanding Younger Actress: Heather Tom (VICTORIA NEWMAN)

Outstanding Directing Team

Outstanding Art Direction/Set Decoration/Scenic Design

Outstanding Technical Direction/Electronic Camera/Video Control

Outstanding Live and Direct to Tape Sound Mixing

Nominations

Outstanding Daytime Drama Series

Outstanding Actor:

Peter Bergman (JACK ABBOTT) and Eric Braeden (VICTOR NEWMAN)

Outstanding Actress:

Jeanne Cooper (KATHERINE CHANCELLOR)
and Melody Thomas Scott (NIKKI NEWMAN)

Outstanding Supporting Actor:

Kristoff St. John (NEIL WINTERS) and Christian LeBlanc (MICHAEL BALDWIN)

Outstanding Younger Actor:

Joshua Morrow (NICHOLAS NEWMAN) and Bryant Jones (NATHAN HASTINGS)

Outstanding Younger Actress:

Camryn Grimes (CASSIE NEWMAN) and Ashley Jones (MEGAN DENNISON)

Outstanding Writing Team

And the Soap Opera Award Goes to . . .

ALTHOUGH *The Young and the Restless* has remained the number one ranked soap opera for the past eleven years, the readers of *Soap Opera Digest* have yet to vote it Favorite Soap Opera. Despite lower ratings, *Days of Our Lives* and *General Hospital* have dominated not only that category but the *Soap Opera Digest* Awards in general, suggesting that the two shows have a far more ardent fan base than *Y&R*. Although the voting system has suffered from accusations of bloc voting, the *Soap Opera Digest* Awards, whose name has been changed several times during its history, remain an important honor for daytime stars. Because the nominees are picked by the magazine's editors, who actually watch the shows, performers tend to be picked for their work in a given year rather than their name recognition. As such, the *Soap Opera Digest* Awards have recognized a number of *Y&R* favorites long overlooked by the Emmy voters such as: Brenda Dickson (JILL FOSTER ABBOTT), Lauralee Bell (CHRISTINE WILLIAMS), and Doug Davidson (PAUL WILLIAMS), who leads the *Y&R* team with four trophies.

SOAPY AWARD WINNERS (1977-83)

In their first incarnation as the Soapys, awards were presented to only two performers from *The Young and the Restless* between the years 1977 and 1983, inclusive. John McCook (LANCE PRENTISS) picked up the very first award for Favorite Male Newcomer. The following year, Brandi Tucker

John McCook (pictured here with wife Laurette Spang)
was voted Favorite Male Newcomer in 1977.

© *Albert Ortega, Moonglow Photos*

(KAREN BECKER) was named Favorite Juvenile Female. In 1981, the editors
presented an Outstanding Achievement in Daytime Award to executive
producer John Conboy.

The 1984 Soap Opera Awards

David Hasselhoff co-hosted the ceremony with his then-wife, Catherine Hickland. Not only did no one from Y&R win any awards, no one placed in the top three runners-up in any category.

1985 Soap Opera Awards

Instead of the top four vote-getters, the top five were now listed. *The Young and the Restless* still didn't win the top spot, but it at least placed some names into the final five in three categories. Creator and head writer Bill Bell was presented with the Editor's Award for Continuing Contribution to Daytime Drama. Hasselhoff and Hickland were back again to co-host the ceremony.

Exciting New Actor, 2nd place:
Phil Morris (TYRONE JACKSON)

Outstanding Actress in a Mature Role, 4th place:
Jeanne Cooper (KATHERINE CHANCELLOR)

Outstanding Villain, 5th place:
Terry Lester (JACK ABBOTT)

Outstanding Daytime Serial: 5th place

1986 Soap Opera Awards

The voting rules changed. Rather than let fans vote for whomever they pleased, the editors narrowed the field to a limited list of nominees. Terry Lester was up for awards in two categories (lead actor and villain) but walked away empty-handed. The lead actor race found Lester competing against his onscreen nemesis Eric Braeden (VICTOR NEWMAN). It was one of three races that found Y&R cast mates pitted against one another.

Winners

Outstanding Actress in a Supporting Role:
Jeanne Cooper (KATHERINE CHANCELLOR)

Nominations

Outstanding Daytime Serial

Outstanding Lead Actor:
Eric Braeden (VICTOR NEWMAN) and Terry Lester (JACK ABBOTT)

Outstanding Lead Actress: Eileen Davidson (ASHLEY ABBOTT)

Outstanding Younger Leading Actor:
Michael Damian (DANNY ROMALOTTI) and Doug Davidson (PAUL WILLIAMS)

Outstanding Younger Leading Actress:
Tracey E. Bregman (LAUREN FENMORE) and Beth Maitland (TRACI ABBOTT)

Outstanding Villain: Terry Lester (JACK ABBOTT)

Outstanding Villainess: Brenda Dickson (JILL ABBOTT)

1988 SOAP OPERA AWARDS

No awards were presented in 1987 so that the ceremony could be shifted from an end-of-the-year event to a beginning-of-the-year event. For the first and only time in the ceremony's history, two actors were nominated for playing the same role, albeit in different categories. Brenda Dickson (JILL ABBOTT) won the best villain award after being fired from the show; her replacement, Jess Walton, was nominated as lead actress.

Winners

Outstanding Villainess: Brenda Dickson (JILL ABBOTT)

Nominations

Outstanding Daytime Soap

Outstanding Lead Actor:
Eric Braeden (VICTOR NEWMAN) and Terry Lester (JACK ABBOTT)

Outstanding Lead Actress:
Jeanne Cooper (KATHERINE CHANCELLOR) and Jess Walton (JILL ABBOTT)

Outstanding Hero: Doug Davidson (PAUL WILLIAMS)

Outstanding Heroine: Eileen Davidson (ASHLEY ABBOTT)

Outstanding Supporting Actress: Tricia Cast (NINA WEBSTER)

1989 SOAP OPERA AWARDS

1989 belonged to longtime Y&R star Jeanne Cooper. Not only did she win the award for lead actress, she also picked up the coveted Editor's Award. Her family, including L.A. Law star Corbin Bernsen, turned out to see her honored.

Winners
Outstanding Lead Actress: Jeanne Cooper (KATHERINE CHANCELLOR)

Outstanding Lead Actor: Eric Braeden (VICTOR NEWMAN)

Outstanding Supporting Actor: Quinn Redeker (REX STERLING)

Nominations
Outstanding Daytime Soap

Outstanding Villainess:
Tricia Cast (NINA WEBSTER) and Jess Walton (JILL ABBOTT)

1990 SOAP OPERA AWARDS

A few months after quitting the role of Jack Abbott and joining *Santa Barbara*, Terry Lester co-hosted this year's ceremony. The editors of *Soap Opera Digest* were obviously quite taken with Nina Webster's (Tricia Cast) transformation from villainess to heroine. One year after being nominated as best villainess, Cast moved into the heroine category. Nina's onscreen transformation earned the show a nomination for best storyline.

Winners
Outstanding Hero: Doug Davidson (PAUL WILLIAMS)

Nominations
Outstanding Daytime Soap

Outstanding Lead Actor: Eric Braeden (VICTOR NEWMAN)

Outstanding Lead Actress: Jeanne Cooper (KATHERINE CHANCELLOR)

Outstanding Heroine: Tricia Cast (NINA WEBSTER CHANCELLOR)

Outstanding Villainess: Barbara Crampton (LEANNE LOVE)

Outstanding Storyline: Nina's transformation into a heroine

1991 SOAP OPERA AWARDS

Doug Davidson became the first actor on the show to pick up two *Soap Opera Digest* Awards, which he did in back-to-back years.

Winners

Outstanding Hero: Doug Davidson (PAUL WILLIAMS)

Nominations

Outstanding Daytime Soap

Outstanding Lead Actor: Eric Braeden (VICTOR NEWMAN)

Outstanding Lead Actress: Melody Thomas Scott (NIKKI NEWMAN)

1992 SOAP OPERA DIGEST AWARDS

Bill Bell picked up his second Editors' Award while Doug Davidson picked up his third award, this time as supporting actor.

Winners

Outstanding Supporting Actor: Doug Davidson (PAUL WILLIAMS)

Outstanding Younger Leading Actress:
Tricia Cast (NINA WEBSTER CHANCELLOR)

Nominations

Outstanding Daytime Soap Opera

Outstanding Female Newcomer: Victoria Rowell (DRUCILLA BARBER)

Best Wedding: Danny and Cricket

Best Love Story: Jack and Nikki

1993 SOAP OPERA DIGEST AWARDS

Kimberlin Brown (SHEILA CARTER) became the first, and so far only, actor to be nominated for playing the same character on two different shows in a given year. Just as Peter Bergman had won the Emmy that eluded his predecessor Terry Lester, so too did he pick up the *Soap Opera Digest* Award for lead actor, an award for which Lester had twice been nominated. The outstanding storyline category was changed to "social issue storyline," for which Cricket's sexual harrassment lawsuit was recognized.

Winners

Outstanding Lead Actor: Peter Bergman (JACK ABBOTT)

Outstanding Villain/Villainess: Kimberlin Brown (SHEILA CARTER)

Nominations

Outstanding Daytime Soap

Hottest Male Star: Eric Braeden (VICTOR NEWMAN)

Hottest Female Star: Tracey Bregman-Recht (LAUREN FENMORE)

Outstanding Younger Leading Actor: Scott Reeves (RYAN MCNEIL)

Outstanding Younger Leading Actress: Heather Tom (VICTORIA NEWMAN)

Outstanding Social Issue Storyline: Cricket's sexual harrassment suit

Favorite Song: "Starting Here, Starting Now" (Danny and Cricket's theme)

1994 SOAP OPERA DIGEST AWARDS

Although the outstanding newcomer category is normally peopled by performers in their teens and early twenties, senior citizen Maxine Stuart (MARGARET ANDERSON) snagged a nomination. Jess Walton won the Lead Actress Award, making Jill Abbott one of the few roles to earn awards for two performers. The social issue storyline category reverted back to simply "best storyline," and Victor Newman's presumed death earned a nomination.

Winners
Outstanding Lead Actress: Jess Walton (JILL FOSTER ABBOTT)

Outstanding Younger Leading Actor: Scott Reeves (RYAN MCNEIL)

Outstanding Scene Stealer: Victoria Rowell (DRUCILLA BARBER)

Nominations
Outstanding Daytime Soap

Outstanding Lead Actor: Peter Bergman (JACK ABBOTT)

Hottest Male Star: Eric Braeden (VICTOR NEWMAN)

Hottest Female Star: Melody Thomas Scott (NIKKI REED NEWMAN)

Outstanding Younger Leading Actress: Heather Tom (VICTORIA NEWMAN)

Outstanding Male Newcomer: Paul Walker (BRANDON COLLINS)

Outstanding Female Newcomer: Maxine Stuart (MARGARET ANDERSON)

Outstanding Child Actor: John Alden (NICHOLAS NEWMAN)

Favorite Storyline: Victor's presumed death

1995 SOAP OPERA DIGEST AWARDS
Nominees were reduced to three per category. Victoria Rowell, who was nominated for Hottest Female Star, co-hosted the ceremony with John Laroquette. Signy Coleman, who won the Supporting Actress Award, was written off the show several months later.

Winners
Outstanding Supporting Actress: Signy Coleman (HOPE ADAMS NEWMAN)

Nominations
Outstanding Daytime Soap

Outstanding Lead Actress: Melody Thomas Scott (NIKKI NEWMAN)

Hottest Female Star: Victoria Rowell (DRUCILLA WINTERS)

Outstanding Male Newcomer: Philip Moon (KEEMO VOLIEN ABBOTT)

Outstanding Child Actor: Courtland Mead (PHILLIP CHANCELLOR IV)

1996 SOAP OPERA DIGEST AWARDS

The Awards ceremony this year was held on Valentine's Day. Joshua Morrow (NICHOLAS NEWMAN) gave his award to his mother as a gift.

Winners

Outstanding Younger Lead Actor: Joshua Morrow (NICHOLAS NEWMAN)

Outstanding Female Newcomer: Michelle Stafford (PHYLLIS ROMALOTTI)

**Joshua Morrow is all smiles after receiving
a *Soap Opera Digest* Award.**
© *Albert Ortega, Moonglow Photos*

Outstanding Daytime Soap

Outstanding Lead Actress: Jess Walton (JILL FOSTER ABBOTT)

Outstanding Younger Lead Actress: Lauralee Bell (CHRISTINE WILLIAMS)

1997 SOAP OPERA AWARDS

Michelle Stafford, who had recently left *Y&R*, was let off from a night shoot of her new primetime serial *Pacific Palisades* to attend the ceremony and, as it turned out, pick up her second award. Eric Braeden also picked up his second award. Doug Davidson won his fourth, putting him in the lead among his cast mates.

Winners

Outstanding Lead Actor: Eric Braeden (VICTOR NEWMAN)

Outstanding Supporting Actor: Doug Davidson (PAUL WILLIAMS)

Outstanding Villainess: Michelle Stafford (PHYLLIS ROMALOTTI)

Outstanding Younger Lead Actress: Heather Tom (VICTORIA NEWMAN)

Nominations

Outstanding Daytime Soap

Hottest Romance: Nick and Sharon

1998 SOAP OPERA AWARDS

Some people felt that Lauralee Bell, who was pushing thirty at the time, had been nominated in the wrong category as Outstanding Young Actress.

Winners

Hottest Female Star: Sharon Case (SHARON NEWMAN)

Outstanding Female Newcomer: Sabryn Genet (TRICIA DENNISON)

Doug Davidson picked up his fourth
Soap Opera Digest Award in 1997.

© *Albert Ortega, Moonglow Photos*

Outstanding Daytime Soap

Hottest Male Star: Shemar Moore (MALCOLM WINTERS)

Outstanding Supporting Actress: Tricia Cast (NINA WEBSTER MCNEIL)

Outstanding Young Actress: Lauralee Bell (CHRISTINE WILLIAMS)

1999 SOAP OPERA AWARDS

Lauralee Bell moved from the Young Leading Actress category into the Supporting Actress category and won her first *Soap Opera Digest* Award, the only one *Y&R* would receive this year.

Winners

Outstanding Supporting Actress: Lauralee Bell (CHRISTINE WILLIAMS)

Nominations

Outstanding Daytime Soap

Outstanding Lead Actor: Eric Braeden (VICTOR NEWMAN)

Hottest Male Star: Shemar Moore (MALCOLM WINTERS)

Outstanding Younger Actor: Scott Reeves (RYAN MCNEIL)

Favorite Return: Christian LeBlanc (MICHAEL BALDWIN)

THE ULTIMATE *YOUNG AND THE RESTLESS* QUIZ

Around Genoa City

1. What is the closest major city to Genoa City?
- (a) Los Angeles
- (b) New York
- (c) Chicago
- (d) Toronto

2. What was the name of the newspaper Stuart Brooks published?
- (a) *Genoa City Herald*
- (b) *Genoa City Examiner*
- (c) *Genoa City Chronicle*
- (d) *Genoa City Times*

3. What was the name of Derek Thurston's beauty parlor?
- (a) The Cutting Edge
- (b) The Golden Comb
- (c) The New Woman Salon
- (d) The Glamorama

4. Into what sanitarium was Katherine Chancellor committed?
- (a) Fairview
- (b) Bayview
- (c) Ferncliff
- (d) Oak Haven

5. What is the main product sold at Crimson Lights?
- (a) alcohol
- (b) clothing
- (c) coffee
- (d) diamonds

By the Book

6. Which Brooks sister penned *In My Sister's Shadow?*
- (a) Leslie
- (b) Lorie
- (c) Chris
- (d) Peggy

7. What was the title of Traci Abbott's first novel?
- (a) *Valley of Regret*
- (b) *Little Sister*
- (c) *Echoes of the Past*
- (d) *Restless Youth*

8. Which of Victor Newman's wives wrote *Victor Newman: The Man, The Myth?*

(a) Julia Bennett

(b) Leanna Randolph

(c) Hope Adams

(d) Nikki Reed

9. To whom did Cole Howard dedicate his first novel?

(a) Victoria

(b) Nikki

(c) Victor

(d) his mother, Eve

10. About whom was the biography *Ruthless* written?

(a) Jack Abbott

(b) Jill Foster Abbott

(c) David Kimble

(d) Victor Newman

Before Viagra

11. When Phillip Chancellor couldn't make love to Katherine, she responded by reciting what?

(a) the Lord's Prayer

(b) the Serenity Prayer

(c) their wedding vows

(d) the alphabet

12. What was the first name of Cassandra Rawlins's rich but impotent husband?

(a) Albert

(b) Tyler

(c) George

(d) Edmund

13. Which character was left impotent after being harpooned?

(a) Lance Prentiss

(b) Lucas Prentiss

(c) Nathan Hastings

(d) Victor Newman

14. How was Paul Williams rendered unable to perform?

(a) He was shot.

(b) He was hit by a car.

(c) His medication had a side effect on him.

(d) He caught Christine in bed with Danny.

15. John Abbott's bout with impotence drove his wife Jill into an affair with whom?

(a) Jed Sanders

(c) Jack Abbott

(b) John Silva

(d) Victor Newman

Striptease

16. What was the name of the club where Nikki stripped for a living?

(a) Avalon

(c) The Club

(b) The Bayou

(d) Derek's Place

17. What was the name of the male stripper who became Katherine Chancellor's paid escort?

(a) Patrick Baker

(c) Jerry Cashman

(b) Felipe Ramirez

(d) Wayne Addison

18. What was the name of the porno film in which Boobsie Caswell was a body double for Nikki?

(a) *Hot Hips*

(c) *Naughty Nikki*

(b) *Long Legs*

(d) *Nikki Needs a New Man*

19. From what did Paul Williams's nude centerfold force him to resign?

(a) the Genoa City Council

(b) the Big Brother Program

(c) the governor's council on pornography

(d) the Holy Name Society at his church

20. What was the name of the magazine for which Victoria Newman agreed to pose nude?

(a) *Yes*

(c) *Playthings*

(b) *Men's View*

(d) *Esprit de Corps*

Miscellaneous

21. Which of the Brooks sisters was not Stuart Brooks's biological child?

(a) Leslie

(b) Lorie

(c) Chris

(d) Peggy

22. Why did Vanessa Prentiss wear a veil all the time?

(a) She didn't want Stuart Brooks to recognize her.

(b) Her face had been burned in a fire.

(c) She liked the way it unnerved people.

(d) She'd picked up the custom while living in the Middle East.

23. What was the name of the cult that Nikki Reed joined?

(a) The New World Commune

(b) Children for Peace

(c) Tranquility Farm

(d) The Enlightenment Center

24. What cartoon character did Flo Webster dress as for the Masquerade Ball?

(a) The Little Mermaid

(b) Little Orphan Annie

(c) Marge Simpson

(d) Wonder Woman

25. As an inside joke, murderer David Kimble demanded at gunpoint that a plastic surgeon give him what TV star's face?

(a) Y&R alumnus David Hasselhoff

(b) Y&R alumnus Tom Selleck

(c) Ronn Moss, who plays Ridge Forrester on *The Bold and the Beautiful*

(d) "that guy from *The Innocent Years*"

Bonus Question #1

What Michael Keaton comedy included a Y&R clip featuring Melody Thomas Scott as Nikki?

(a) *Beetlejuice*

(b) *Mr. Mom*

(c) *Night Shift*

(d) *Multiplicity*

Bonus Question #2

What unusual character from another show got hooked on Y&R?

(a) Marlena Evans while possessed by Satan (*Days of Our Lives*)

(b) Timmy the doll brought to life (*Passions*)

(c) Casey the alien from another planet (*General Hospital*)

(d) Reva's clone (*Guiding Light*)

Cast List

ACTOR ROLE

Robert Ackerman	JOHN HARDING (1981)
Wanda Acuna	KEESHA MONROE (1994–95)
Deborah Adair	JILL FOSTER ABBOTT (1980–83)
Marla Adams	DINA MERGERON (1983–86, 1991, 1996)
Sarah Aldrich	VICTORIA NEWMAN (1997)
Marilyn Alex	MOLLY CARTER (1991–93, 1995)
Morey Amsterdam	MOREY (1989–90)
Alicia Anderson	SARAH COSTNER (1997)
Beverly Archer	SHIRLEY SHERWOOD (1999)
Tisha Arning	SASHA GREEN (1995–97)
Rod Arrants	JEFF THE STABLEBOY (1974)
	DR. STEVEN LASSITER (1986–88)
Nina Arvesen	CASSANDRA RAWLINS (1988–91)
Pamela Bach	MARI JO MASON (1994)
Parley Baer	MILES DUGAN (1993–96)
Diana Barton	MARI JO MASON (1994–96)
Peter Barton	DR. SCOTT GRAINGER (1988–93)

Ashley Bashioum	MACKENZIE REYNOLDS (1999–present)
William H. Bassett	PETE WALKER (1982–83)
Jaime Lyn Bauer	LORIE BROOKS PRENTISS (1973–82, 1984)
Fred Beir	MITCHELL SHERMAN (1975)
Lauralee Bell	CHRISTINE "CRICKET" BLAIR WILLIAMS (1983–present)
Frank M. Benard	MARC MERGERON (1983–84, 1987–88)
Nick Benedict	MICHAEL SCOTT (1980–81)
Meg Bennett	JULIA NEWMAN (1980–84, 1986)
Marcus Bentley	CHUCKIE ROULLAND (1981–82)
Peter Bergman	JACK ABBOTT (1989–present)
Carlos Bernard	RAFAEL DELGADO (1999–present)
Thom Bierdz	PHILLIP CHANCELLOR III (1986–89)
Beau Billingslea	TRENT JORDAN (1995)
Dick Billingsley	PHILLIP CHANCELLOR III (1981)
Laura Bryan Birn	LYNNE BASSETT (1988–present)
Vasili Bogazianos	AL FENTON (1998–99)
Jay Bontatibus	TONY VISCARDI (1999–2000)
Eric Braeden	VICTOR NEWMAN (1980–present)
Robin Braxton	LILLIE BELLE BARBER (1994)
Tracey E. Bregman	LAUREN FENMORE (1983–95)
Angelle Brooks	DR. STEPHANIE SIMMONS (1996)
David Allen Brooks	KEITH DENNISON (1999)
Randy Brooks	NATHAN HASTINGS (1992–93)
Candy Ann Brown	SALENA WILEY (1990)
Kimberlin Brown	SHEILA CARTER (1990–93, 1995)

Jaime Lyn Bauer was an original cast member.

© *Albert Ortega, Moonglow Photos*

Peter Brown ROBERT LAURENCE (1981–82)

Susan Brown FRAN WHITAKER (1975)

Woody Brown JAKE LOPEZ (1996)

Karl Bruck MAESTRO ERNESTO FAUSTCH (1974–82)

Brendan Burns GLENN RICHARDS (1989, 1991–93, 1995–96)

Barry Cahill SAM POWERS (1974–75)

Steve Carlson DR. MARK HENDERSON (1975–76)

Andi Carnick RACHEL LONG (1997)

Paul Carr MARTIN GANTRY (1986–89)

Cathy Carricaburu NANCY BECKER (1977–78)

Charles Carroll DR. BRUCE HENDERSON (1975)

Sharon Case SHARON COLLINS NEWMAN (1994–present)

Colleen Casey FARREN CONNOR (1985–87)

Tricia Cast NINA WEBSTER MCNEIL (1986–present)

John Castellanos JOHN SILVA (1989–present)

Christine McCall Champion JERI PAULSEN (1995)

Loyita Chapel JUDY WILSON (1980–81)

Lilyan Chauvin MARIANNE ROULLAND (1974)

LIL (1989–90)

Colby Chester MICHAEL CRAWFORD (1985–89)

Nathaniel Christian LENNY WILKENS (1982)

Eddie Cibrian MATT CLARK (1994–96)

Robert Clary PIERRE ROULLAND (1973–74)

Tamara Clatterbuck ALICE JOHNSON (1998–present)

Robert Colbert STUART BROOKS (1973–83)

Dennis Cole LANCE PRENTISS (1981–82)

Signy Coleman HOPE ADAMS NEWMAN (1993–97)

Scott Combs TIMOTHY O'KEEFE (1984)

Darlene Conley ROSE DEVILLE (1979–80, 1986–87)

John Considine PHILLIP CHANCELLOR II (1973–74)

Carolyn Conwell MARY WILLIAMS (1980–present)

Jeanne Cooper KATHERINE CHANCELLOR STERLING (1973–present)

MARGE COTROOKE (1989–90)

Jeff Cooper DEREK THURSTON (1976)

Glenn Corbett JAMES LAKE (1983)

Michael Corbett DAVID KIMBLE (1986–91)

Melinda Cordell DOROTHY STEVENS (1980–83)

MADAME ESTELLE CHAUVIN (1990–94)

David Cowgill CLIFF WILSON (1993–96)

Grant Cramer SHAWN GARRETT (1984–86)

ADAM HUNTER (1996)

Barbara Crampton LEANNE LOVE (1987–93, 1998–present)

Lee Crawford SALLY MCGUIRE (1973–74, 1981–82)

Steven Culp BRIAN HAMILTON (1995)

Todd Curtis SKIP EVANS (1987–91)

Abby Dalton LYDIA SUMMERS (1995)

Candice Daly VERONICA LANDERS (1997–98)

Michael Damian DANNY ROMALOTTI (1981–98)

Kenneth Danziger HENRY (1997)

Jeanne Cooper is the show's longest running cast member.

© *Albert Ortega, Moonglow Photos*

Doug Davidson PAUL WILLIAMS (1978–present)

Eileen Davidson ASHLEY ABBOTT (1982–88, 1999–present)

Josie Davis GRACE TURNER (1996–97)

Kristine DeBell PAM WARREN (1982)

Lee DeBroux JOHN HARDING (1981–82)

Dick DeCoit RON BECKER (1976–77, 1984)

Marita DeLeon JOANI GARZA (1995–present)

Alex Demir WES O'CONNELL (1995)

John Denos JOE BLAIR (1983–87)

Mark Derwin ADRIAN HUNTER (1989–90)

Charles DeVries MAX (1982)

Don Diamont BRAD CARLTON (1985–96, 1998–present)

Brenda Dickson JILL FOSTER ABBOTT (1973–80, 1983–87)

Linda Dona LINDA COSTNER (1997)

Norma Donaldson LILLIE BELLE BARBER (1990–94)

Alex Donnelley DIANE JENKINS NEWMAN
(1982–86, 1996–present)

Jerry Douglas JOHN ABBOTT (1982–present)

Brenda Epperson Doumani ASHLEY ABBOTT (1988–96)

Phil Dozois FRANK BARRITT (1995, 1997)

Cynthia [Eilbacher] Jordan APRIL STEVENS LYNCH (1979–82, 1992–94)

William Grey Espy DR. WILLIAM "SNAPPER" FOSTER (1973–75)

Andrea Evans PATTY WILLIAMS ABBOTT (1983–84)

Michael Evans COLONEL DOUGLAS AUSTIN
(1980–85, 1987–95)

Patricia Everly PEGGY BROOKS (1979)

Sharon Farrell	FLO WEBSTER (1991–present)
Jonathan Farwell	GEORGE RAWLINS (1988–89)
Cindy Fisher	REBECCA (1980)
	DANA (1987)
Steven Ford	ANDY RICHARDS (1981–87)
Vivica A. Fox	DR. STEPHANIE SIMMONS (1995)
David Sharke Fralick	"WART" WARTON (1995–96, 1999–2000)
Helen Funai	SUMIKO (1980)
Jennifer Gareis	GRACE TURNER (1997–99)
Joy Garrett	BOOBSIE CASWELL AUSTIN (1983–85)
Kelly Garrison	REBECCA HARPER (1990)
	HILLARY LANCASTER (1990–92)
Jennifer Gatti	KEESHA MONROE (1995–96)
Anthony Geary	GEORGE CURTIS (1973)
Sabryn Genet	KELLY (1995)
	TRICIA DENNISON MCNEIL (1997–present)
Amy Gibson	ALANA ANTHONY (1985)
John Gibson	JERRY "CASH" CASHMAN (1981–82)
Robert Gibson	DAVID MALLORY (1981)
Bond Gideon	JILL FOSTER (1980)
Siena Goines	CALLIE ROGERS (1999–present)
Ricky Paull Goldin	GARY DAWSON (1999–present)
Justin Gorence	PETER GARRETT (1996–98)
Charles Gray	WILLIAM FOSTER SR. (1975–76)
Velekka Gray	DR. SHARON REAVES (1983)
	RUBY (1983–84)

Dorothy Green   JENNIFER BROOKS (1973–77)

James Michael Gregory   CLINT RADISON (1989–90)

Stephen Gregory   CHASE BENSON (1988–91)

Camryn Grimes   CASSIE NEWMAN (1997–present)

Bennet Guillory   WALTER BARBER (1992–94)

Brett Hadley   CARL WILLIAMS (1980–90, 1998)

Mark Haining   NORM PETERSON (1994)

Deidre Hall   BARBARA ANDERSON (1973–75)

Tom Hallick   DR. BRAD ELIOT (1973–78)

Brett Halsey   JOHN ABBOTT (1980–82)

Lynn Harbaug   LISA MANSFIELD (1988–89)

Fawne Harriman   MARGARET LAKE (1983)

David Hasselhoff   DR. WILLIAM "SNAPPER" FOSTER (1975–82)

Fay Hauser   SALENA WILEY (1984, 1986, 1989–91, 1996–97)

Wings Hauser   GREG FOSTER (1977–81)

Thomas Havens   MATTHEW (1980)

Susan Seaforth Hayes   JOANNA MANNING (1984–89)

Kay Heberle   JOANN CURTIS (1975–78)

Karen Hensel   DORIS COLLINS (1994–present)

Anthony Herrera   JACK CURTIS (1975–77)

Christopher Holder   KEVIN BANCROFT (1981–83)

Randy Holland   RICK DAROS (1983–84)

Erica Hope   NIKKI REED (1978–79)

James Houghton   GREG FOSTER (1973–76)

Brody Hutzler   CODY (1999–present)

James Ivy	JEREMY ROSS (1997)
Gladys Jiminez	RAMONA CACARES (1999–present)
Ashley Jones	MEGAN DENNISON (1997–present)
Bryant Jones	NATE HASTINGS (1996–present)
Jennifer Karr	ELLEN WINTERS (1986–87)
Beau Kazer	BROCK REYNOLDS (1974–80, 1984–86, 1988–92, 1999–present)
Liz Keifer	ANGELA LAURENCE (1982–83)
Brian Kerwin	GREG FOSTER (1976–77)
Andre Khabbazi	ALEC MORETTI (1997–98)
Amelia Kinkade	VIVIAN (1990)
Heath Kizzier	DR. JOSHUA LANDERS (1996–98)
Kari Kupcinet	JULIE SANDERSON (1991)
Spencer Klass	VICTOR NEWMAN JR. (1996)
Lauren Koslow	LINDSEY WELLS (1984–86)
Bert Kramer	BRENT DAVIS (1984–85)
Christopher Kriesa	DR. SCOTT ALLEN (1995–96)
Jerry Lacy	JONAS (1979–81)
Joe LaDue	DEREK THURSTON (1977–80, 1984)
David Lago	RAUL (1999–present)
Sal Landi	CLINT RADISON (1989)
Charlie Lang	DR. TERRY ARCHER (1997)
Katherine Kelly Lang	GRETCHEN (1981)
Greg Lauren	BRETT NELSON (1999–present)
John Phillip Law	DR. JIM GRAINGER (1988–89)
Adam Lazarre-White	NATHAN HASTINGS (1994–96)

Jennifer Leak	GWEN SHERMAN (1974–75)
Scotty Leavenworth	BILLY ABBOTT (1996–98)
Christian LeBlanc	MICHAEL BALDWIN (1991–93, 1997–present)
Roberta Leighton	DR. CASEY REED (1978–81, 1984–87, 1998)
Terry Lester	JACK ABBOTT (1980–89)
Victoria-Ann Lewis	DORIS COLLINS (1994)
Tom Ligon	LUCAS PRENTISS (1978–82)
Kate Linder	ESTHER VALENTINE (1982–present)
Tracy Lindsey	VERONICA LANDERS (1997)
Alex D. Linz	PHILLIP CHANCELLOR IV (1995)
Stephen Liska	DETECTIVE JOE LACERRA (1998)
William Long Jr.	WAYNE STEVENS (1980–82)
Aaron Lustig	DR. TIMOTHY REID (1996–98)
Janice Lynde	LESLIE BROOKS (1973–77)
Beth Maitland	TRACI ABBOTT (1982–96, 1999)
Victoria Mallory	LESLIE BROOKS PRENTISS (1977–82, 1984)
Heidi Mark	SHARON COLLINS (1994)
Margaret Mason	EVE HOWARD (1980–84, 1993)
Neal Matarazzo	DETECTIVE MARLO EDMUNDS (1998)
Brian Matthews	ERIC GARRISON (1983–85)
Mimi Maynard	CAROLYN HARPER (1982)
Julianna McCarthy	LIZ FOSTER (1973–88, 1993)
Leigh J. McCloskey	KURT COSTNER (1996–97)
Tom McConnell	SHAWN GARRETT (1984)
John McCook	LANCE PRENTISS (1976–80)

Howard McGillin GREG FOSTER (1981–82)

Dorothy McGuire CORA MILLER (1984)

Dawn McMillan DRUCILLA WINTERS (1996)

Jim McMullan BRENT DAVIS (1984)

Terrence E. McNally ROBERT LYNCH (1993–94)

Courtland Mead PHILLIP CHANCELLOR IV (1993–95)

Ernestine Mercer MILLIE JOHNSON (1997–99)

Freeman Michaels DRAKE BELSON (1995–96)

Jeanna Michaels KAREN RICHARDS (1981–82)

Kerry Leigh Michaels MICHELLE SANDERSON (1991)

Ashley Nicole Millan VICTORIA NEWMAN (1982–91)

William Mims SAM POWERS (1973)

Victor Mohica FELIPE RAMIREZ (1980–81)

Philip Moon KEEMO VOLIEN ABBOTT (1995–96)

Allan Dean Moore SERGEANT RAYMOND KING (1994–96)

Shemar Moore MALCOLM WINTERS (1994–present)

Melissa Morgan BRITTANY NORMAN (1988–90)

Julianne Morris AMY WILSON (1994–96)

Phil Morris TYRONE JACKSON (1984–86)

Joshua Morrow NICHOLAS NEWMAN (1994–present)

Conci Nelson HEATHER STEVENS LYNCH (1993–94)

Sandra Nelson PHYLLIS SUMMERS ROMALOTTI (1997–98)

Jill Newton MELISSA DAROS (1983)

Lee Nichol SVEN (1985)

John O'Hurley DR. JIM GRAINGER (1989–91)

Amy O'Neill MOLLIE (1986)

Ken Olandt DEREK STUART (1988–89)

Scott Palmer TIM SULLIVAN (1983–87)

Nicholas Pappone PHILLIP CHANCELLOR MCNEIL (1996–present)

Robert Parucha Matt Miller (1985–87)

Patsy Pease PATRICIA FENNELL (1996)

J. Eddie Peck COLE HOWARD (1993–99)

Anthony Peña MIGUEL RODRIGUEZ (1984–present)

Larry Pennell JUDGE CHET ASHFORD (1997)

Brock Peters COMMANDER FRANK LEWIS (1982–89)

Joe Petracek TINY (1988–89)

Devon Pierce DIANE WESTIN (1990–91)

Drew Pillsbury DAVID KIMBLE (1986)

Monica Potter SHARON COLLINS (1994)

Nathan Purdee NATHAN "KONG" HASTINGS (1985–92)

Francesco Quinn TOMAS DEL CERRO (1999–present)

Kelli Rabke BERNADETTE ROGERS (1993, 1995)

Betty Rae BETTY ARNOLD (1990–97)

Logan Ramsey JOSEPH ANTHONY (1984–85)

Marguerite Ray MAMIE JOHNSON (1982–90)

Alex Rebar VINCE HOLLIDAY (1979–80, 1986–87)

Veronica Redd MAMIE JOHNSON (1990–95, 1999–present)

Quinn K. Redeker NICK REED (1979)

REX STERLING (1987–94)

Marianne Rees MAI VOLIEN (1994–96)

Scott Reeves RYAN MCNEIL (1991–present)

Donnelly Rhodes PHILLIP CHANCELLOR II (1974–76)

Lynn Richter	CHRIS BROOKS FOSTER (1979–82)
Deanna Robbins	CINDY LAKE (1982–83)
Josh Michael Rose	BILLY ABBOTT (1995–96)
Victoria Rowell	DRUCILLA BARBER WINTERS (1990–98, 2000–present)
JoDean Russo	REGINA HENDERSON (1975–76)
Jon St. Elwood	JAZZ JACKSON (1983–86)
Christopher St. John	REVEREND GREER (1991–93, 1995–97)
Kristoff St. John	NEIL WINTERS (1991–present)
Henry G. Sanders	WALTER BARBER (1991)
Lanna Sanders	BETTY ANDREWS (1974–75)
Isabel Sanford	JUDGE ELLEN BETHANY (1996)
Paul Savior	WALTER ADDISON (1980)
Beth Scheffel	BARBARA ANN HARDIN (1981–82)
Joe Sciacca	WALLY (1991)
Melody Thomas Scott	NIKKI REED NEWMAN (1979–present)
Robin Scott	AMY WILSON (1994)
Nick Scotti	TONY VISCARDI (1996–99)
Tom Selleck	JED ANDREWS (1974–75)
Shari Shattuck	ASHLEY ABBOTT (1996–98)
John Shearin	EVAN SANDERSON (1986–87)
Mary Sheldon	NAN (1989–90)
Shane Silver	BILLY ABBOTT (1993–95)
Marc Singer	CHET (1999)
Doug Sloan	JEFF (1990)
Pamela Peters Solow	PEGGY BROOKS (1973–81, 1984)

Michelle Stafford	PHYLLIS SUMMERS ROMALOTTI (1994–97)
Warren Stanhope	REVEREND DANIELS (1988, 1989, 1991, 1992)
Douglas Stark	REVEREND MALLORY (1985)
Jack Stauffer	SCOTT ADAMS (1979)
Trisha Sterling	PAM WARREN (1982)
Lilibet Stern	PATTY WILLIAMS ABBOTT (1980–83)
K. T. Stevens	VANESSA PRENTISS (1976–80)
Paul Stevens	DR. BRUCE HENDERSON (1975–76)
Trish Stewart	CHRIS BROOKS FOSTER (1973–78, 1984)
Caleb Stoddard	DEREK THURSTON (1976)
James Storm	NEIL FENMORE (1983–86)
Carl Strano	MAX (1983)
Rebecca Street	JESSICA BLAIR (1988–89)
Duke Stroud	GEORGE SUMMERS (1995)
Charlotte Stuart	TAMRA (1986)
Maxine Stuart	MARGARET ANDERSON (1993–96)
Elizabeth Sung	LUAN VOLIEN ABBOTT (1994–96)
Hayden Tank	VICTOR NEWMAN JR. (1996–97)
Mark Tapscott	EARL BANCROFT (1982–83)
Joseph Taylor	TONY DISALVO (1982–83)
Josh Taylor	JED SANDERS (1993–94)
Tammi Taylor	PATTY WILLIAMS (1980)
Christopher Templeton	CAROL ROBBINS EVANS (1983–93)
Michelle Thomas	CALLIE ROGERS (1998)
Gordon Thomson	PATRICK BAKER (1997–98)

Terrence Tierney   TINY (1989–90)

Michael Toland   KEVIN ANDREWS (1997)

David Tom   BILLY ABBOTT (1999–present)

Heather Tom   VICTORIA NEWMAN (1991–present)

Sandra Torres   BENITA LOPEZ (1996)

Constance Towers   AUDREY NORTH (1996)

Brandi Tucker   KAREN BECKER (1977–78)

Paul Tulley   EDWARD (1981)

Michael Tylo   ALEX "BLADE" BLADESON (1992–95)

RICK BLADESON (1994–95)

Granville Van Dusen   KEITH DENNISON (1996–98, 2000–present)

Rodney Van Johnson   TREY STARK (1998–99)

John Vargas   RANDALL RAMOS (1997)

Neil Vipond   RAYMOND BECKER (1997)

Nicholas Walker   JASON MONROE (1988)

Paul Walker   BRANDON COLLINS (1993)

William A. Wallace   BRIAN HAMILTON (1997)

Jess Walton   JILL FOSTER ABBOTT (1987–present)

Vernee Watson-Johnson   BIRDIE (1999–present)

Patty Weaver   GINA ROMA (1982–present)

Doug Wert   JEFF (1990)

Ellen Weston   SUZANNE LYNCH (1979–80)

Forest Whitaker   NATHAN "KONG" HASTINGS (1984)

Tom Whyte   GRANT LONG (1997)

Stephanie Williams   AMY LEWIS (1983–88)

Tonya Lee Williams   DR. OLIVIA BARBER WINTERS (1990–present)

David Winn STEVE WILLIAMS (1980)

William Wintersole MITCHELL SHERMAN (1986–present)

Janet Wood APRIL STEVENS (1979)

Lynn Wood STEVE WILLIAMS (1981–83)

Greg Wrangler DR. JIM PETERSON (1992)

STEVE CONNELLY (1992–96)

Carmen Zapata SISTER THERESA (1975)

Suzanne Zenor CLAIRE LAURENCE (1982)

Bibliography

Bonderoff, Jason. *Soap Opera Babylon*. New York: Putman, 1987.

Cassata, Mary and Barbara Irwin. *The Young and the Restless: Most Memorable Moments*. Santa Monica: General Publishing Group, 1996.

Hyatt, Wesley. *The Encyclopedia of Daytime Television*. New York: Billboard Books, 1997.

Irwin, Barbara and Mary Cassata. *The Young and the Restless: Special Silver Anniversary Collector's Edition*. Santa Monica: General Publishing Group, 1998.

LaGuardia, Robert. *Soap World*. New York: Arbor House, 1983.

Lofman, Ron. *Celebrity Vocals*. Iola, WI: Krause Publications, 1994.

McNeil, Alex. *Total Television: A Comprehensive Guide to Programming from 1948 to the Present,* 4th edition. New York: Penguin, 1996.

O'Neil,Thomas. *The Emmys: Showdowns, Star Wars and the Supreme Test of TV's Best*. New York: Penguin, 1992.

Rout, Nancy E., Ellen Buckley, and Barney Rout (editors). *The Soap Opera Book: Who's Who in Daytime Drama*. West Nyack, NY: Todd Publications, 1992.

Schemering, Christopher. *The Soap Opera Encyclopedia,* 2nd edition. New York: Ballantine, 1987.

Waggett, Gerard J. *The Soap Opera Book of Lists.* New York: HarperCollins, 1996.

———.*The Soap Opera Encyclopedia.* New York: HarperCollins, 1997.

Whitburn, Joel. *The Billboard Book of Top 40 Hits.* New York: Billboard Publications, Inc., 1989.

My research also relied on back issues of *Soap Opera Weekly, Soap Opera Digest, Soap Opera Magazine, Soap Opera News, Soaps in Depth, Soap Opera Update,* and *TV Guide.*

Answers to Quizzes

WHEN DID YOU GET HERE?

1. Jill Foster Abbott (March 1973); 2. Katherine Chancellor (late 1973); 3. Paul Williams (1978); 4. Victor Newman (1980); 5. Diane Jenkins Newman (1982); 6. Christine Blair Williams (1983); 7. Miguel Rodriguez (1984); 8. Nina Webster McNeil (1986); 9. Ryan McNeil (1991); 10. Malcolm Winters (1994)

OUT OF THE NIGHT

1. (a) *Rat Patrol*; 2. (c) Robert Clary; 3. (d) *Laredo* and *The Lawman*; 4. (b) *The Bad News Bears*; 5. (d) Don Diamont; 6. (a) *Mama's Family*; 7. (c) *The Powers of Matthew Star*; 8. (d) Zorro; 9. (c) *Charles in Charge*; 10. (b) Michelle Thomas (CALLIE ROGERS)

GENOA CITY'S TEN MOST WANTED LIST

1. Rose DeVille; 2. Sven; 3. Leanna Love; 4. Shawn Garrett; 5. Matt Clark; 6. Lisa Mansfield; 7. David Kimble; 8. Sheila Carter; 9. Joseph Anthony; 10. Veronica Landers

AKA

1. (b) William; 2. (b) Nathan Hastings; 3. (c) Rex Sterling; 4. (b) Robert Tyrone; 5. (d) Leanna Randolph; 6. (c) Charles; 7. (a) Jim Adams; 8. (b) Jim Bradley; 9. (a) Sarah; 10. (d) Victor Newman

Isn't It Romantic?

1. (a) Chris refused to have sex until the wedding night; 2. (c) in his hospital room; 3. (c) Lance's mother, Vanessa; 4. (b) "Through the Eyes of Love" from *Ice Castles*; 5. (c) shoplifting; 6. (d) gardener; 7. (b) He was an alcoholic; 8. (b) her brother, Scott Grainger; 9. (a) Drucilla wanted Olivia's boyfriend, Nathan; 10. (c) Noah

When They Were Young

1. (h) Tony Geary/GEORGE CURTIS; 2. (g) Deidre Hall/BARBARA ANDERSON; 3. (d) Mark Derwin/ADRIAN HUNTER; 4 (a) Liz Keifer/ANGELA LAURENCE; 5. (b) Granville Van Dusen/KEITH DENNISON; 6 (c) Kimberlin Brown/SHEILA CARTER; 7. (j) Rodney Van Johnson/TREY STARK; 8. (e) Lauren Koslow/LINDSEY WELLS; 9. (f) John McCook/LANCE PRENTISS; 10. (i) Darlene Conley/ROSE DEVILLE

Before They Were Young

1. (d) Don Diamont/CARLO FORENZA, *Days of Our Lives*; 2. (e) Eileen Davidson/KELLY CAPWELL, *Santa Barbara*; 3. (h) Peter Bergman/DR. CLIFF WARNER, *All My Children*; 4. (a) Sharon Case/DEBBIE SIMON, *As the World Turns*; 5. (j) Ricky Paull Goldin/DEAN FRAME, *Another World*; 6. (i) Tricia Cast/CHRISTY DUVALL, *Santa Barbara*; 7. (b) Christian LeBlanc/KIRK McCOLL, *As the World Turns*; 8. (g) Jess Walton/SHELLEY GRANGER, *Capitol*; 9. (f) Kristoff St. John/ADAM MARSHALL, *Generations*; 10. (c) Patty Weaver/TRISH CLAYTON, *Days of Our Lives*

The Ultimate Young and the Restless Quiz

1. (c) Chicago; 2. (c) *Genoa City Chronicle;* 3. (b) The Golden Comb; 4. (a) Fairview; 5. (c) coffee; 6. (b) Lorie; 7. (c) *Echoes of the Past;* 8. (b) Leanna Randolph; 9. (b) Nikki; 10. (d) Victor Newman; 11. (a) The Lord's Prayer; 12. (c) George; 13. (d) Victor Newman; 14. (b) He was hit by a car; 15. (a) Jed Sanders; 16. (b) The Bayou;

17. (c) Jerry Cashman; 18. (a) *Hot Hips;* 19. (c) the governor's council on pornography; 20. (d) *Esprit de Corps;* 21. (b) Lorie; 22. (b) Her face had been burned in a fire; 23. (a) The New World Commune; 24. (b) Little Orphan Annie; 25. (a) *Y&R* alumnus David Hasselhoff; Bonus Question Number One: (b) *Mr. Mom;* Bonus Question Number Two: (d) Reva's clone on *Guiding Light.*

Index

Page numbers in **bold** indicate photographs.

About the Author

A LEADING authority on soap operas, Gerard J. Waggett
has authored nine books on the genre, including *The Ultimate Days of
Our Lives Trivia Book* (Renaissance, 1999), *The Ultimate Another World
Trivia Book* (Renaissance, 1999), *The Soap Opera Encyclopedia*, and *The
Soap Opera Book of Lists*. He has written about soap operas for numerous
publications, including *Soap Opera Weekly, Soap Opera Update, Soaps In
Depth*, and *TV Guide*. He is a graduate of Harvard College and holds a
master's degree in English from the University of Massachusetts. He
resides in Dorchester, Massachusetts.

also available from

RENAISSANCE BOOKS

The Ultimate Days of Our Lives Trivia Book
by Gerard J. Waggett
ISBN: 1-58063-049-9 • $9.95

The Ultimate Another World Trivia Book
by Gerard J. Waggett
ISBN: 1-58063-081-2 • $9.95

Daytime Divas
The Dish on Dozens of Daytime TV's Great Ladies
by Kathleen Tracy
ISBN: 1-58063-087-1 • $14.95

From Soap Stars to Superstars
Celebrities Who Started Out in Daytime Drama
by Annette D'Agostino
ISBN: 1-58063-075-8 • $14.95

TO ORDER PLEASE CALL
1-800-452-5589

BOOKS